SECRET
VANCOUVER

SECRET VANCOUVER

The Unique Guidebook to Vancouver's Hidden Sites, Sounds, & Tastes

2010 Edition

Alison Appelbe

WITH PHOTOGRAPHS BY
Linda Rutenberg

ECW PRESS

NATIONAL LIBRARY OF CANADA CATALOGUING IN PUBLICATION DATA

Appelbe, Alison
Secret Vancouver 2010 : the unique guidebook to Vancouver's hidden sites, sounds & tastes
/ Alison Appelbe.

Includes index.
ISBN-13: 978-1-55022-911-0 / ISBN-10: 1-55022-911-7

1. Vancouver (B.C.) — Guidebooks. I. Title.

FC3847.18.A67 2009   917.11 33045   C2009-903037-3

Original series design: Paul Davies / Series editor: Laura Byrne Paquet.
Typesetting: Martel *en-tête* / Imaging: Guylaine Régimbald – SOLO DESIGN.
Cover design: Tania Craan
Front cover image: Yves Marcoux / Getty Images
Printing: Webcom   1   2   3   4   5

Mixed Sources
Product group from well-managed
forests, and other controlled sources
www.fsc.org Cert no. SW-COC-002358
© 1996 Forest Stewardship Council
FSC

Published by ECW PRESS
2120 Queen Street East, Suite 200, Toronto, Ontario M4E 1E2.
416.694.3348 / info@ecwpress.com

The publication of *Secret Vancouver 2010* has been generously supported by the Government of
Canada through the Book Publishing Industry Development Program (BPIDP).

Canadä

PRINTED AND BOUND IN CANADA

ECW PRESS
ecwpress.com

TABLE OF CONTENTS

Introduction 9

How to Use *Secret Vancouver* 10

Acknowledgments 11

SECRET...

INTRODUCTION

Some time ago, a Canadian journalist working in Hong Kong told me that Asians viewed Vancouver as little more than "a puddle" on the far side of the North Pacific. Also quiet, and boring, he added for my edification. Then this city's co-director of planning described Vancouver as a "postage stamp of a city" when it comes to the larger scheme of things.

They are both right. Vancouver is small by global standards — roughly 2.2 million people if you include the entire metropolitan area. And it's a fair distance from the hot political and cultural centers of the world. This may be a disadvantage, but it also works in our favor. The same planner also sees Vancouver as a "sanctuary city," and I think that just about sums it up. Vancouver is peaceable, lush, clean, affluent, and relatively safe.

A strength is obviously its natural setting. The city is shaped around a gorgeous inlet with mountains to the north, and a tremendous river to the south. And while admittedly it rains a lot, the climate is temperate enough to make it ideal for year-round outdoor activity. Hey, mountain biking (covered in this guide) was practically born on the North Shore.

Another plus is the people who've settled here in the past quarter century. Building on a largely (though not exclusively) European population, hundreds of thousands of Asian immigrants — particularly Chinese-speakers from Southeast Asia, but also a large contingent from the Indian subcontinent — have added a dimension that can't be undervalued or underestimated; they've made this city an immensely more attractive and interesting place.

Finally, Vancouver is shaping up to be one of the best examples of New Urbanism in North America. This movement aims to make inner cities livable again, and attract at least some suburbanites back to the denser, richer atmosphere of the central city. It's happening. Residential growth on Vancouver's downtown peninsula — from False Creek through the Downtown South to Coal Harbour — is far exceeding expectations.

This guide is intended to help you explore these and other lesser-known facets of this city — deliberately omitting the clichés and tourist traps such as the Capilano Suspension Bridge (wonderful though the canyon is), overpriced Robson Street, and the Gastown Steam Clock. In short, it's meant to get you off the tourist track, below the surface, and into the places and cultures that make Vancouver really livable. Travel (by electric trolley bus or passenger ferry), dig deep, walk, explore, talk to the locals — dance with them, for that matter. Above all, enjoy yourself. There's more to this city than its good bones.

HOW TO USE SECRET VANCOUVER

Secret Vancouver's topics are listed alphabetically. The best way to use the guide is to browse the topics in the index, get a sense of how it works, and pursue your interests. If you're looking for gelato or Japanese food, for example, it's straightforward. But you may have to dig into sections on, say, books, clubs, gardens, or bistros for the information, ambiance, or entertainment you're after. There are several topics devoted to helping you see the city at its best — or, more accurately, most real. These include Enclaves, Asian malls, Hollyburn, Kitsilano,

Outlooks, Chinatown, and Rough and Seedy. Finally, there are the city's small eccentricities — such as raccoons, blackberries, volleyball, and *feng shui*.

Most attractions include a street address and phone number. Hours of operation, entrance fees, and other ever-changing facts of life are omitted in the interest of remaining as up to date as possible, and conserving space. Change is perpetual, of course, and a few of these sites may have bitten the dust before you read about them. My advice: call ahead if you have any doubts. Also note that Vancouver phone numbers have ten digits; you have to dial the area code, even when making a local call. On the few occasions that money is mentioned, it's in Canadian currency (weak though it is).

Finally, use the city's newspapers to update yourself on local happenings. The *Vancouver Sun* and *Vancouver Province* both contain good weekly events listings, and the city's many free publications, listed under "Secret Alternative Media," are a similarly rich source of current information. It should also be noted that this guide is not intended to be anywhere near exhaustive. There are features of this city that deserve to be included, and aren't. And there are those that will raise the question: Why the heck did she mention that? Rather, the goal is to give you some help in moving beyond the obvious.

ACKNOWLEDGMENTS

I'd be remiss if I didn't credit several sources and individuals for helping me put this guide together. Not a day passed that I didn't learn more about the city from our daily and community newspapers. And I often referred to an incredible tome assembled by editor Chuck Davis, *The Greater Vancouver Book*. Though much has changed since it was published in 1997, it remains an invaluable source on the history, and breadth and depth, of the city.

Finally, I'd like to thank a handful of people who were particularly generous with information, or went out of their way to help me out. They include Kaleena Sessions, Jean Sorensen, Richard Bice, Ken Buhay, Frank Appelbe, Heather Persons, Stephanie Taggart, Sylvia Talbot, Diana King, and Terri Clark. And particularly my brother Trent, who proofread the manuscript.

SECRET

ABORIGINAL ART
❖

Coastal Peoples Fine Arts Gallery (1024 Mainland Street, Yaletown, 604-685-9298) represents First Nations artists from the Queen Charlotte Islands, Alert Bay, and other communities along the coast. In a gallery-like store, it shows and sells bentwood boxes, ceremonial masks, totem poles, argillite carvings, and jewelry, as well as Inuit carvings, cards, and books.

In 1946, Lloyd and Frances Hill acquired a general store and post office at Koksilah on central Vancouver Island and began selling the work of local natives there. Today, they claim to represent more than 1,000 Northwest artists at five locations in the province. **Hill's Native Art** (165 Water Street, Gastown, 604-685-4249, www. hillsnativeart. com) carries genuine Cowichan sweaters, each numbered and associated with a particular knitter, and similarly certified masks, baskets, jewelry, and argillite by coastal natives. As well, Hill's has a fine collection of Inuit carvings in bone and soapstone. And in a third-floor gallery, you'll find totem poles, bentwood boxes, button blankets, and ceremonial masks of extraordinary complexity and drama. **Leona Lattimer** (1590 West 2nd Avenue, Kitsilano, 603-732-4556) has long shown and sold fine native Indian pieces. A long-time dealer and collector in Inuit and regional native art is Ron Appleton of **Appleton Galleries** (1451 Hornby Street, Downtown South, 604-685-1715).

The spacious **Inuit Gallery** (206 Cambie Street, Gastown, 604-688-7323, www.inuit.com) also handles Northwest Coast native art, specializing in sculpture, bone, prints, drawings, and tapestries from the Far North. It's here you'll see the works of some of the most celebrated Inuit carvers.

North Vancouver remains home to Squamish people, some of whom live on the Capilano reserve. Among them is the Baker family, which operates the **Khot-La Cha Art Gallery and Gift Shop** (270 Whonoak Street, North Vancouver, 604-987-3339). The shop is located in traditional Capilano territory, just southeast of Marine Drive and Capilano Road.

This is an opportunity to talk with the people who have used and made these products for generations. While they sell cedar poles, prints, jewelry, and Cowichan sweaters, their specialty is hand-tanned moosehide crafts and porcupine quill and bone jewelry.

A somewhat out-of-the-way surprise is the collection of carvings and jewelry at a store best known for its camping supplies, the **Three Vets** (2200 Yukon Street, Central Vancouver, 604-872-5475).

SECRET

ABORIGINAL ATTRACTIONS

In a just few years, native-operated tourism has become a force in B.C., and the **Aboriginal Tourism Association of British Columbia** (www.aboriginalbc.com, 604-921-1070, 1-877-266-2822) is an excellent source. Businesses run by indigenous peoples province-wide embrace opportunities to visit their ancestral terrain, interact, and watch them at work. Natives make award-winning wines, and run championship golf courses. They oversee world-class galleries and, of course, operate adventure tours and wildlife viewing into unimaginably remote regions. Numerous native-owned lodges, casinos, RV parks and heritage villages are listed on the website.

SECRET

AFRICAN

There's no ethnic community in the world unrepresented in Vancouver, and Somalis and Ethiopians are here in fair numbers. Somalis run small businesses in the Broadway and Fraser Street area, and on a short stretch of Commercial Drive north of the new SkyTrain mega-station on Broadway. Eateries include the **Addis Café** (2017 Commercial Drive, East Vancouver, 604-254-1929) and **Harambe Ethiopian Cuisine** (2149 Commercial Drive, East Vancouver, 604-216-1060). Both prepare a stir-fry called Awaze tibs — beef, lamb, or chicken enlivened with spices and eaten with a flatbread called injera. Interestingly, injera is made with an indigenous Ethiopian grain. Both restaurants also serve vegetarian and bean dishes.

Nyala African Cuisine is a long-time restaurant with a warm atmosphere and "pan-African" menu of tapas and entrées that runs from boerewors kabobs (skewered sausages) to Yedoro Infille (poultry, with a serious hot sauce) (4148 Main Street, East Vancouver, 604-876-9919).

SECRET

AIRPORT

Vancouver International Airport (Richmond, 604-207-7077, www.yvr.ca) is a destination in its own right: it routinely makes top-ten lists of world airports compiled by air-related organizations and by major magazines such as *Condé Nast Traveler*. Little wonder. Close to one billion dollars has been spent over the past decade in creating an outdoorsy, if Modernist, environment that suggests the province's lush coastal habitat while highlighting its indigenous native culture. For the most part it works — spectacularly (but then again, a major US airline executive told me that behind the good looks, there are lingering problems).

The International Terminal collection of First Nations art is first rate. Coming into the arrivals hall, you encounter two giant *Welcome Figures* and a *Spindle Whorl* of red cedar, both by Salish artist Susan Point. In fact, the sculpture appears in regular waves, complemented by colorful hanging weavings by members of the Vancouver-based Musqueam band.

But the airport's pièce de résistance is Bill Reid's *Spirit of Haida Gwaii: The Jade Canoe*, located in the International Terminal's departures lounge. This shimmering bronze sculpture is a 20-by-13-by-11.5-foot paean to a cast of rogues who paddled the coast — and fantastic enough, in every sense of the word, to keep this airport on the mental map of many of the 17.5 million passengers who pass through annually.

On the windows behind *The Jade Canoe* extends *The Great Wave Wall* by Lutz Haufschild. Inspired by the Great Wave of Kanagawa by

Japanese artist Hokusai, this massive piece of light and glass suggests a "lyrical ocean realm."

With the 2010 Winter Olympic Games and opening of the **Canada Line** rapid transit system (www.canadaline.ca) between downtown Vancouver and the airport, the number of passengers will reach 19 million.

As to the many stores (lots of smoked salmon and outdoor wear), restaurants, and bars, management demands street pricing — meaning you shouldn't pay more than you would on (expensive) Robson Street.

Absolute Spa has locations in both the international (604-270-4772) and domestic (604-273-4772) departures halls, and the airport's **Fairmont Hotel** (604-248-2772). Here, you can find relief for those fear-tense shoulders or revel in a full body treatment, if time allows.

Outside the International Terminal, you'll find **Chester Johnson Park** — with benches, totems, and walking path — in which to relax and regain your composure after losing your luggage, missing your flight, leaving your spouse, etc.

SECRET

AL FRESCO

After a long winter of rolling black clouds, if not steady rain, any slight sign of that big yellow ball in the sky does funny things to people here.

(Actually, a lot of Vancouverites wear shorts and sandals year-round — whether as a demonstration of their hardiness or connection with the wild, or as a perennial act of wishful thinking, I can't say. This type also tends to eat outside, year-round, in their woolly sweaters and Gore-Tex jackets.)

But back to the general population. When a wan April sun appears, worshippers head for the beach, doffing their clothes in temperatures they wouldn't tolerate in their own homes. Come May, everyone wants to dine outside. Suddenly, you can't find a seat on the southwest-facing patio at Kits Coffee, and the waterfront deck at Bridges on Granville Island begins to look crowded. Why? In part, because Vancouverites like to think of themselves as slightly European. Bottom line: summer is short. Al fresco dining is very big.

There is outside, and then there is *outside*. Any food business that can claw from the city a little bit of rented sidewalk space will put out some tables and chairs and call it a patio. This is fine if you don't mind ingesting diesel fumes with your meal, and putting up with barking dogs chained to the lamppost. Conditions are better on side roads like Yew Street in Kitsilano, where, though patios are usually small, there is less traffic.

But the best al fresco dining happens where a true patio or courtyard exists. A favorite is **Brix** (1138 Homer Street, Yaletown, 604-915-9463). This funky space with an interior courtyard serves some heady entrées, but simpler tapas as well. There are also sixty or so wines by the glass.

If you climb the open staircase inside **Joe Fortes Seafood and Chop House** (777 Thurlow Street, Downtown, 604-669-1940), you'll arrive at a spacious patio where the fashionable and flush hang out.

Some of the best outdoor dining is found along the concrete loading docks that once served the railway — at the warehouses-turned-restaurants and bars of Yaletown. Dine in peace, even splendor (food-and ambiance-wise), at the **Blue Water Café and Raw Bar** (1095 Hamilton Street, 604-688-8078); **Cioppino's Mediterranean Grill** (1133 Hamilton Street, 604-688-7466); and **Simply Thai Restaurant** (1211 Hamilton Street, 604-642-0123).

The second-storey modernist **Watermark** "on kits beach" is arguably the ultimate outdoor location, with a 180-seat patio (enclosed when the weather acts up) and stunning views up Burrard Inlet. Serving contemporary West Coast cuisine, and with a good wine list, it's open daily for lunch and dinner, and for weekend brunches (1305 Arbutus Street, in Kitsilano Beach Park, Kitsilano, 604-738-5487). A good (unrelated) take-out operates at the sidewalk level.

Less hip, but as visually sensational, are the patios at **Sequoia Grill at the Teahouse Restaurant** at Ferguson Point (7501 Stanley Park Drive, Stanley Park, 604-669-3281) and the well-regarded **Fish House in Stanley Park** (8901 Stanley Park Drive, near the tennis courts, 604-681-7275). Another gorgeous patio space (with interesting food) is located in a Modernist building overlooking Howe Sound that once served as the University of British Columbia (UBC) Faculty Club — **Sage Bistro** (6331 Crescent Road, UBC, 604-822-0968).

Great views of False Creek can be had from **Monk McQueen's Oyster and Seafood Bar** (601 Stamps Landing, Central Vancouver, 604-877-1351) and **Sandbar** — a multi-faceted restaurant complex with separate sushi bar and heated patio dining (1535 Johnston Street, Granville Island, 604-669-9030). North False Creek also boasts some exceptional patios (and restaurants), including upper-register **C Restaurant** (1600 Howe Street, Downtown South, 604-681-1164). However, city ordinances demanded by nearby residents require some mid-evening patio closures here, I'm told.

Alternatively, observe the passing madness along The Drive (where life pulsates into the wee hours) from the patio of the youngish and trendy **Havana** (1212 Commercial Drive, East Vancouver, 604-253-9119). **The Cannery Seafood House** (2205 Commissioner Street, East Vancouver, 604-254-9606) provides picture-window views of marine activity on inner Burrard Inlet, along with excellent seafood. Note: the Cannery (www.canneryseafood.com) will relocate in 2010 to make way for Port of Vancouver expansion.

Further afield, there's the comfy **Beach House at Dundarave Pier** (150 25th Street, West Vancouver, 604-922-1414), located right on the wave-battered shoreline. Or travel by gondola up Grouse Mountain to the heady **Observatory** (North Vancouver, 604-984-0661), housed in a rustic, comfy chalet. South of the city, and popular with the burger and beer crowd, is the **Flying Beaver Bar** on the Fraser River (4760 Inglis Drive, Richmond, 604-273-0278).

One of the best al fresco sites in the city is the **Galley Patio and Grill** (1300 Discovery Street, Westside, 604-222-1331) in the Jericho Sailing Centre. Food-wise, it's mostly paddler-size breakfasts, burgers, and fish 'n' chips. In its own words, it's "perched directly over the sand of Locarno Beach...with views across English Bay to the majestic North Shore mountains and east to Vancouver's magnificent skyline"—a pretty accurate pitch for the setting. On the downside, the Galley is only open on weekends from fall to spring, though daily from May through mid-September.

A superb place for a leisurely and peaceful lunch is the terrace of the **Gallery Café**, above the Vancouver Art Gallery (750 Hornby Street, Downtown, 604-688-2233).

SECRET

ALTERNATIVE MEDIA

The *Georgia Straight* (604-730-7000, www.straight.com), a longtime free-distribution weekly paper, remains at the top of the heap of Vancouver's so-called community or urban papers. If holding a paper so well endowed with advertising doesn't tire your arms, you'll find much of interest. The abundance of advertising, coupled with respect for editorial, means the paper pays decently enough to attract good freelancers.

The *Straight* leans heavily to entertainment. It is particularly strong on the alternative music, club, film, and theater scenes, although even the so-called serious arts get decent treatment. Eating and cooking (in and out), clothing and related vanities, books, the outdoors, travel — and distinctly left-leaning politics — are all here. The paper hits business foyers, public facilities such as libraries, and sidewalk boxes on Thursdays.

The thrice-weekly *Vancouver Courier* (604-738-1411, www.canada .com/vanouvercourier) has been around for eons, delivering in-depth coverage of civic politics and neighborhood disputes. The *West Ender*, another long-timer, delivers news and entertainment to the West End.

Broadcasting from the depths of the Downtown Eastside, **Vancouver Cooperative Radio** (better known as Co-op Radio), at 102.7 FM, remains a strong non-commercial voice and well-loved source of off-the-map music and comment — social, political, and otherwise.

Unbeknownst to many people, Vancouver has no fewer than three Chinese-language daily newspapers — all owned in Asia, but printed here, with some overseas wire copy. *Sing Tao* and *Ming Pao* are read by Cantonese- and Mandarin-speaking Chinese, and have large, local editorial staffs. The *World Journal* is published for the local Taiwanese population.

S E C R E T

ANTIQUES
⚜

Vancouver's upscale South Granville neighborhood between the north end of the Granville bridge and West 16th Avenue is sprinkled with antique shops (and art galleries). Among them is **Panache Antiques**, specializing in 17th to 19th century antique furniture (2229 Granville Street, Central Vancouver, 604-732-1206). As well, a stretch of Granville Street in the south of the city (the Marpole area) has antique stores, as does Main Street, between 12th and 30th avenues.

Generic country stuff is the perennial rage, and one of the better outlets is **Farmhouse Collections** (2915 Granville Street, Central Vancouver, 604-738-0167). Here, alongside the furniture, you'll find the usual wrought-iron roosters, but also rust-mesh hanging cone baskets and a great selection of rustic pails, bins, and vases.

You're into a totally other realm at **Architectural Antiques** (2403 Main Street, East Vancouver, 604-872-3131). Its grandiose pieces appear in movies; the movie stars occasionally shop here for costly eccentricities. The store ceiling drips with antique lamps, the walls with sconces. The large premises also carries over-the-top period furniture, mantelpieces, and larger-than-life stained glass.

Actually, antiques and Main Street are synonymous all the way south to East 33rd Avenue. **Baker's Dozen Antiques** (3520 Main Street, East Vancouver, 604-879-3348) carries Western Canadian pioneer and native collectibles, crafts, artwork, and knickknacks. But most of the practical furniture is found in an uneven mixture of ever-evolving stores on Main Street south of King Edward Avenue (technically East 25th Avenue). Vintage pinball machines and jukeboxes are refurbished and sold at **John's Jukes** (2343 Main Street, East Vancouver, 604-872-5757).

SECRET

AROMATHERAPY

Unsurprisingly, Vancouver has proved fertile ground for this approach to soothing and healing, and a B.C.–based business, **Escents Aromatherapy**, operates across Canada to Taiwan (including, in Vancouver, 2579 West Broadway, Kitsilano, 604-736-7761 and 1744 Commercial Drive East Vancouver, 604-639-9494 — the latter with a basic spa). The defining service of these and similar aromatherapy outfits is the blending of "essential oils" to fit your personality and desires. For example, a blend of lavender and geranium is said to relax, while oils of Asiatic trees, such as *ylang-ylang* and patchouli, are associated with sensuality. Massage oils, such as a "rejuvenating" blend of rind of grapefruit and bergamot, are also available.

Saje (Nature's Remedies and Aromatherapy) also has a number of outlets. There's a particularly warm atmosphere at the Saje I'm familiar with (2252 West 4th Avenue, Kitsilano, 604-738-7253, www. saje.ca). As well as all the essential oils, this outlet stocks books and playful gift items. It also does something called Sit-Taj or "seated aromatherapy massage."

To my way of thinking, perfume falls into the aromatherapy category, and **The Perfume Shoppe** in the Sinclair Centre (226–757 West Hastings Street, Downtown, 604-299-8463) pursues perfumes that nobody else stocks. It has as many as 1,000 scents I'm told by a knowing perfume consumer, including rare perfumes from countries other than major producers such as France. In pursuit of a coriander scent for a relative (I can't imagine it either), he found it here.

S E C R E T

ART GLASS

Ian Tan operates the **ian tan gallery** of contemporary Canadian art (2202 Granville Street, Central Vancouver, 604-738-1077, www.iantangallery.com). While paintings figure largely in his collection, he also champions the art-glass scene. An interest in the West Coast glass-art scene has grown, in part, from the Pilchuk School of glass art in Washington state and the work of Seattle-area superstar Dale Chihuly. Associated with these American trendsetters, Western Canada has developed its own community of glass artists, though they are "regrettably better known in the us than in Canada," says Tan.

To witness glass being blown in an industrial setting, go to **Robert Held Art Glass**, a huge blue corrugated iron warehouse (2130 Pine Street, Kitsilano, 604-737-0020). You can watch the guys from the street, carefully inserting their fledging creations in the fiery-orange glory hole. Inside the building, you can examine the results on wooden racks and the best of the pieces in an adjacent shop. Perfectly respectable "seconds" make inexpensive gifts.

Smaller, but no less notable, **Andrighetti Glassworks** (3 West 3rd Avenue, Kitsilano, 604-731-8652) produces some way-out pieces, including gorgeous long-stem glasses, often with a humorous or arty twist. And, though it's certainly no secret, the **New-Small & Sterling Studio Glass** (1440 Old Bridge Street, Granville Island, 604-681-6730) functions as both performance gallery and well-appointed art glass emporium.

S E C R E T

ARTHUR ERICKSON

Vancouver is known architecturally for the hundreds of Arts-and-Crafts- and Craftsman-style mansions and bungalows built early in the twentieth century, the smallest of which now fetches a handsome price. Notable for their shingle exteriors, brick chimneys, stained glass, natural-stone bases, and interior woodwork, they're found throughout the west side, but particularly on the leafy streets of upscale Shaughnessy, Kerrisdale, Kitsilano, and West Point Grey.

But the greatest period of design in this city was between 1930 and 1970, when the region was a Western leader of Modernist, Expressionist architecture — particularly in wood-frame post-and-beam houses, characteristically open to the woodsy coastal elements and flooded with natural light.

The best known of the notable architects who pioneered this trend remains the late **Arthur Erickson** (www.arthurerickson.com). He designed many of the region's most celebrated houses, mostly nestled into the rock and forest of West Vancouver.

Erickson also made his mark with the **MacMillan-Bloedel Building** on Georgia Street at Thurlow Street — an impressive, waffle-like concrete structure; the low-rise, slope-roofed **Robson Square and Law Courts** (Downtown, bounded by Robson, Howe, Nelson, and Hornby streets), which includes several levels of cascading water from accessible terraces; and the neo-Grecian **Simon Fraser University** atop Burnaby Mountain.

His name appears on the marquee of UBC's **Koerner Library** and the **Scotia Dance Centre** at Granville and Davie streets (Downtown), both of which have transparent glass façades.

Known for dramatic public statements, **Erickson** created public hysteria by predicting that the population of metro Vancouver (**about 2.2 million today**) would soon reach 10 million. He died in 2009.

SECRET

ARTISAN BREADS

Pane E Formaggio: Artisan Bread & Cheese Shop (4532 West 10th Avenue, Westside, 604-224-1623) will, I hope, still be around when artisan bread is, well, just bread. This is an attractive neo-Italian deli-eatery stocked with pancetta and prosciutto; unpasteurized cow's-milk cheese; tapenades and niçoise-style olives; and superior breads in varieties such as olive, and sun-dried apple and pecan.

The dictionary defines "spelt" as a hardy, mountain-grown predecessor of today's cultivated wheats. Mild nutty-flavored spelt breads, squares, and cookies are made at the **Spelt Bakery**, formerly **Arán Foods** (2141 East Hastings Street, East Vancouver, 604-258-2726, open afternoons only).

Sometimes bakeries arrive on the scene and take over — and this is pretty much the case with **Terra Breads**, which makes chewy, edgy breads with olives, figs, rosemary, cranberries, and the like, and bars and cookies that prove, unfortunately, irresistible. Terra outlets include the **Kitsilano Bakery and Café** (2380 West 4th Avenue, 604-736-1838) and **Granville Island Public Market Bakery** (604-685-3102). (This place also belongs on the "Secret Bakery" list). Terra Breads also runs a stand-alone bakery and café in the light industrial district close to the Millennium Water community on False Creek (53 West 5th Avenue, Central Vancouver, 604-873-8111).

S E C R E T

ASIAN MALLS

Those who yearn to immerse themselves in Asian shopping culture have come to a city with a rich, vibrant commercial life. Every year, thousands of Chinese-speaking immigrants land at Vancouver International Airport and set up house in the adjacent municipality of Richmond — where half the population is now Asian — and beyond. They buy or build a house (in the case of Richmond, on what was once farmland and remains an earthquake-prone jelly of alluvial silt), pick up a Japanese car or two, and head out to one of the several buckets at the end of the North American rainbow — the shopping mall.

Those living in Richmond don't have to go far. Strip malls are sited all over what is actually Lulu Island, many with signs in bold Chinese characters. Mall heaven is located in the city's commercial heart — roughly bounded by No. 3 Road and Alderbridge Way (north of Lansdowne Park Shopping Centre), Hazelbridge Way, and Capstan Way.

Over six or seven city-sized blocks you'll find a network of malls that keep morphing into more malls. The whole area has become one sprawling mecca that hints at both sweatshop-dominated Guangzhou (from which many immigrants have come) and a ground-level version of Tokyo's hyper-commercial Shinjuku district.

These malls include early-comer **Yaohan Centre** (with a pan-Asian character), **President Plaza** (catering mostly to Taiwanese), **Aberdeen Centre** (Hong-Kong-ish, chic and upscale, and including the popular, budget Japanese **Daiso** department store), **Parker Place** (the oldest of the malls, with a good food court), **Central Square**, **Empire Square**, and others. Within, individual merchants sell dried everything; most shipable edibles are also available at the huge T&T supermarket in President Plaza, and the Osaka supermarket in the Yaohan Centre. Most include a food court that dishes out regional Chinese and (ever-popular) Japanese, Thai, Korean, and Indian foods. In Aberdeen Centre, you'll find a traditional Chinese tea counter. Across the way in President Plaza, a bakery sells delicacies such as egg-yolk-with-lotus-seed puffs and chestnut tarts. There are stalls devoted to Japanese junk food, and Chinese herbal medicine shops to repair your stomach. Sandwiched into and between the malls are mostly new and fashionable restaurants serving more upscale Asian fare, particularly along Alexandra Road.

Innumerable hole-in-the-wall clothing stores lean to cheap, fashion-of-the-minute apparel popular with Japanese and Hong Kong teenagers. Shoes run to outrageously chunky and pointy black ankle boots; women's items include pigskin purses and glittery sweaters with pseudo-fur collars. A few outlets stock higher-end clothes by names such as Gianfranco Ferre and Versace.

Here you'll also find Chinese-language videos, books, and magazines; imported watches, gems, and jewelry; lower-end electronic equipment and gadgets; even Asian-style photo machines that churn out sentimental prints. Add the wonderful smells and lively crush of an almost exclusively Chinese-speaking crowd and the malls deliver a near-overseas experience.

SECRET

BAGELS

By late on Saturdays, the shelves of **Solly's Bagelry** (189 East 28th Avenue, at Main Street, East Vancouver, 604-872-1821; and 2873 West Broadway, Kitsilano, 604-738-2121) are looking pretty bare — the traditional Jewish bakery is popular. As well as bagels and bagel chips, it sells knishes, poppy-filled folds called hamantaschen, almond mandelbroit, linzertorte, and chocolate-almond meringues.

Siegel's Bagels (1883 Cornwall Avenue, Kitsilano, 604-737-8151; Granville Island Public Market, 604-685-5670) is said to have the proverbial "best bagels." It's also frequented for its Montreal-style smoked meat or brie with red pepper sandwiches. Another reliable bagel shop and Jewish-style eatery is longtime favorite **Max's Bakery and Delicatessen** (3105 Oak Street, 604-733-4838; also 521 West 8th Avenue, 604-873-6297; both in Central Vancouver).

S E C R E T

BAKERIES

Fratelli Authentic Italian Baking (1795 Commercial Drive, East Vancouver, 604-255-8926) makes biscotti, dolce, and St. Honoré, a lavish cream-puff affair named for the patron saint of pastry makers. For a large variety of biscotti and festive cakes such as panettone, another option is the **Calabria Bakery** (5036 Victoria Drive, East Vancouver, 604-324-1337).

In another realm entirely is **Liberty Bakery** (3699 Main Street, East Vancouver, 604-709-9999). It's really a leafy corner coffeehouse filled with idiosyncratic prints and sculpture by the owners' artist daughter and son-in-law. The owners take pride in their traditional Swedish baking, and the community responds. This is a popular meeting place in the SoMa (South Main) area.

Boulangerie La Parisienne (1076 Mainland Street, 604-684-2499) delivers classic French breads and desserts, such as Napoleons, mousse, and limon tarte. Take a window seat and enjoy the Yaletown scene.

At the other end of the dietary spectrum, **Panne Rizo Bakery Café** (1939 Cornwall Avenue, Kitsilano, 604-736-0885, www.pannerizo. com) is a wheat- and gluten-free establishment — a place, says a clerk, where celiacs eat with confidence. It certainly doesn't look or taste deprived: as well as a variety of rice breads and savories, its bakers make rice-based sweets such as butter tarts, macaroons, and berry galettes — even rum balls au chocolat.

Back to convention, a nice little traditional Greek outlet is **Serano Greek Pastry** (3185 West Broadway, Kitsilano, 604-739-3181). If you're like me, you'll look no further than the baklava or kataifi — all dripping with honey — and perhaps the spanakopita (spinach pie).

Both light-filled coffeehouse and bakery, **La Petite France** (2655 Arbutus Street, Kitsilano, 604-734-7844), run by Christian and Anne Ziss, is nicely located at the edge of the recently redeveloped Arbutus industrial lands. A traditional patisserie, it produces both breads and sweet buns, as well as all-stops-out French pastries.

A new kid on the block getting heaps of attention is the **Transilvania Peasant Bakery** (3474 West Broadway, Kitsilano, 604-319-6523). Based on old Romanian recipes (and backed by the local Slow Food movement) this heavy, nutty, yeasty (and not inexpensive) bread is said to merit "a trip right across town."

SECRET

BEACH PARTY

Vancouver is not a swimming city and therefore, in my view, not a beach city (of course, thousands of beachgoers will disagree). In spite of several hundred crazies who scuttle into the frigid waters of English Bay every New Year's Day (and immediately run out again), the ocean water is never particularly inviting. It's saved only by two spectacularly sited open-air (and slightly heated) pools — the salt-water **Kitsilano Pool** (604-731-0011) in Kits Beach Park and the **Second Beach Pool** (604-257-8371) in Stanley Park, both operated by the Vancouver Board of Parks and Recreation.

In East Vancouver, an outdoor freshwater pool designed for family swimming is located in **New Brighton Park**, off McGill Street, north of Hastings Park (604-298-0222). There's also a small children's beach, with a lifeguard, at **Trout Lake** in John Hendry Park, off East 19th Avenue at Victoria Drive.

Wreck Beach (Westside) is something else entirely. More of a culture, really. A long, somewhat ill-defined stretch of rock, logs, and sand around the westernmost extremity of Point Grey, and below the bluffs of UBC, Wreck Beach has been so-called clothing-optional since the 1920s. In summer, it morphs into something of a functioning under-ground economy with food and beer vendors, and people selling neo-hippie clothing (oddly enough) and, presumably, soft drugs.

Politics on the beach can be fierce, and occasionally spills into the newspapers and electronic media (TV loves it, of course): an unsolved murder; worries that the custodians of Pacific Spirit Park, in which Wreck Beach is formally located, are threatening hard-won nudist rights; concern about the perennial erosion of the cliffs above.

Wreck Beach inevitably carries on in its anarchic way. However, this being Canada, it's impossible for even the most regulation-phobic to avoid the long reach of bureaucracy. The latest news I've had is that park officials, in keeping with efforts to manage out-of-control off-leash dog walking (or havoc, or whatever) in the upper reaches of the park, have formally declared a small section of Wreck Beach "off-leash" for nudist pet owners.

That's reason enough to retreat northward to **Spanish Banks** and **Locarno Beach** (Westside). Both are "family beaches," the parks board emphasizes. Actually, it's here that the Vancouver foreshore is at its finest — long stretches of albeit imperfect sand that, when the tide is low, creates shallow pools of toasty water and miniature, temporary aquariums. Best of all is an ocean setting of sailboats leaning in the wind, larger-than-life freighters, and beyond, Howe Sound and the Tantalus and Garibaldi mountain ranges.

On the opposite shore, **Third Beach** (Stanley Park) — reachable from Stanley Park Drive — is fairly secluded, with similarly spectacular outlooks.

Those who equate beaches with privacy might seek out the sandy coves of West Vancouver, usually accessible by lane or path from Marine Drive. A few years back, most of these coveted mini-retreats — at or near **West Bay, Sandy Cove, Caulfeild Cove, Lighthouse Park, Kew Beach,** and **Whytecliff Park** — were marked by concrete signposts at their respective Marine Drive entrances. But some West Van denizens — intent, as always, on keeping out dreaded outsiders — pulled all the posts out. Now you have to find your own way down the defiles and over the rocks, at your relative peril. A friendlier option remains **Belcarra Regional Park** and beach along Indian Arm (out the Barnet Highway at Ioco Road) — where you'll experience still colder water, but a stunning setting on a hot day.

SECRET

BILLIARDS AND BOWLS

✤

I was surprised to learn that Vancouver has forty-odd billiard and pool halls — shows how often I frequent a pool hall. One of the largest is **Guys and Dolls Billiards** (2434 Main Street, East Vancouver, 604-879-4433), boasting "11-9 Ball Gold Crown" and "five Riley snooker tables."

The popular and long-time **Commodore Lanes and Billiards** (838 Granville Street, Downtown, 604-681-1531) is a few steps below street level in the Commodore Ballroom building, smack downtown. The business has 21 tables, a coffee bar and is licensed. A number of Commercial Drive coffeehouses long frequented by Italians and Portuguese have pool tables, including **Joe's Café** (1150 Commercial Drive, East Vancouver, 604-255-1046). Greeks on the west side tend to frequent, with others, **Kitsilano Billiards** (3255 West Broadway, 604-739-9544).

Bowling lives, and aside from the underground Commodore Lanes, there's the five- and ten-pin **Grandview Bowling Lanes** on Commercial Drive, not far from the SkyTrain mega-station (2195 Commercial Drive, East Vancouver, 604-253-2747). And in Kitsilano, the **Varsity-Ridge 5-Pin Bowling Centre** (2120 West 15th Avenue, 604-738-5412) keeps rollin' on.

If your thing is lawn bowling, you'll find one of the most spectacularly sited greens in the world (truly) and congenial players (of all ages) at the **Stanley Park Lawn Bowling Club** (near the park entrance on Beach Avenue, 604-683-0910).

S E C R E T

BISTROS

A newish cluster of restaurants on West Fourth Avenue aren't all bistros per se, but the youthful, laid-back atmosphere (not to mention superb food) promise an a good experience in any of the following: **Bistrot Bistro** (1961 West 4th Avenue, Kitsilano, 604-732-0004, www.bistrotbistro.com); **Fuel** (1944 West 4th Avenue, Kitsilano, 604-288-7905, www.fuelrestaurant.ca) and **Gastropod** (1938 West 4th Avenue, Kitsilano, 604-730-5579, www.gastropod.ca). A caution though, this is not budget bistro-ing.

A knowing friend swears by the steak and fries, and wines, served at **The Smoking Dog** (1889 West 1st Avenue, Kitsilano, 604-732-8811). This Belgian-style bistro boasts a loyal clientele and patio dining in season, at a peaceable location.

A regular goes on about the black-bean soup at **Ouisi Bistro** (3014 Granville Street, Central Vancouver, 604-732-7550), but there's more to this cozy space in upscale South Granville: it's popular for its Louisiana-style dishes, and jazz and blues.

Also on South Granville, squeeze into **Bin 942** (1521 West Broadway, Central Vancouver, 604-734-9421), not much more than a hole in the wall. This eccentric space produces highly unusual tapas, salads, mussels, and other "petit nosh," and has an impressive variety of wines, as does its parent "tapas parlor," **Bin 941** (943 Davie Street, Downtown, 604-683-1246). Both places also have lineups, at last look.

Purists will scoff, but I include here a cluster of licensed restaurants along Main Street in East Vancouver with live music and, in some cases, bars that mock their restaurant licensing (liquor licensing in British Columbia remains vaguely Byzantine). The **Montmartre Café** (4362 Main Street, 604-879-8111) delivers jazz, fusion, world music (local Croatian artists, for example), and poetry readings; the **Cottage Bistro** (4468 Main Street, 604-876-6138) leans to blues, folk, and jazz; and the playful **Locus Café** (1421 Main Street, 604-708-4121) delivers alternative something. Locus's guest book reads, hyperbolically: "a new way of looking at the world."

A bistro-restaurant named one of the best new eateries in Canada by Air Canada's enRoute magazine is **Boneta** (1 West Cordova Street, Gastown, 604-684-1844). Both the décor and the crowd are pretty fancy, and the food (think octopus terrine) and beverages (they make their own ginger beer) in keeping.

Seen by a legion of fans as a genuine bit of bistro Paris, **La Regalade** (2232 Marine Drive, West Vancouver, 604-921-2228) is an easygoing room with an open kitchen. Classic beef bourguignon and coq au vin may well pop up on the menu, along with tarte Tatin. And a place that doesn't claim to be a bistro, but feels bistro to me, is **Café Salade de Fruits** (1545 West 7th Avenue, Central Vancouver, 604-714-5987, www.saladdefruits.com). Maybe it's the simple space, the limited menu, or the barebones (francophone) staff, but here you can expect to dine inexpensively and well on perhaps lamb, duck, or a steamy pan of mussels with fries and mayonnaise. **Burgoo Bistro** (4434 West 10th Avenue, Westside, 604-221-7839), is also recommended for both its ambiance and its food.

SECRET

BLACKBERRIES

Vancouver may be the urban wild blackberry capital of the world. If we've had a hot, dry August (always our best month), the berries produced by this thorny coastal creeper are large, succulent, and plentiful — and, best of all, they're free.

Straight from the vine, they can be tart. Fully sun-ripened and literally falling off the vine, they're usually sweet. With good dollops of sugar, they're indisputably delicious in jams, pies, or blackberry crumble.

You can find blackberries for the picking in a variety of places in Kitsilano, Westside, and South Vancouver. Look for them under the south end of the Burrard Street Bridge, near Vanier Park; west of English Bay along the Stanley Park seawall; and on the railway right-of-way that runs beside Lamey's Mill Road, directly south of Granville Island (watch out for the heritage streetcar). There are also bushes along the walking path just above the foreshore west of Kits Beach, reachable from the foot of Balsam Street or Trafalgar Street, though they may be picked over by the time you arrive.

The native blackberry (trailing blackberry, *Rubus ursinus*) loves logged areas, so you'll find it growing on the higher slopes, often draped and twined over logs and rocks.

But blackberries also gravitate to the Fraser River. Everett Crowley Park (off Kerr Road above Southeast Marine Drive), in the southeast of the city, is apparently so overwhelmed by blackberry bushes that naturalists intent on reclaiming some space for other native species are tearing them out as fast as they can.

While we're onto berries, you might look out for the ubiquitous dwarf huckleberry, a tart-yet-sweet pinkish-red berry that children, particularly on the North Shore, eat in copious quantities. And the dwarf blueberry (blame the latitude) also produces a sweet berry, particularly at the higher altitudes. Modest warning: all these sweets are equally appreciated by brown and black bears.

S E C R E T

BOARDS AND BIKES

Vancouver is something of a skateboarding mecca. *Concrete Powder* magazine (circulation 33,000) claims there are 200,000 boarders between here and Chilliwack in the Fraser Valley.

4th Avenue between Burrard Street and Pine Street (Kitsilano) houses a good chunk of the board-related businesses. The stores are filled with boards of every type (summer and winter) and make, along with bikes designed for extreme sport. Beware Boxing Day lineups.

On the south side of the street, **Westbeach** (1766 West 4th Avenue, 604-731-6449) sells clothes and snowboards — from the plain to the elaborately laminated — and skateboards; on a ramp at the back of the premises, boarders show how it's done. At **Thriller** (3467 Main Street, East Vancouver, 604-736-5651), owner Mike Jackson designs some of his own clothes, the label Grubwear, and boards.

Both ends of the north side of this block boast bike shops. **Ride On Sports** (3469 Main Street, East Vancouver, 604-738-7734, www.rideon.com) specializes in BMX (trick) bikes.

Ride On Again Bikes (2255 West Broadway, Kitsilano, 604-736-7433) has a good selection of refurbished cruisers, road bikes and kids' bikes at reasonable cost.

Westside Sporting Goods Company (118 West Broadway, Central Vancouver, 604-739-4425) is a family-oriented, all-season outfitter of ski and snow-boarding equipment, bikes, backpacks and other camping accessories.

Two kits giants: **The Boardroom** (1745 West 4th Avenue, 604-734-7669, www.boardroomboardshop. com) sells all kinds of snow-boards and skateboards, helmets, sunglasses, even bikinis — if you can handle the rap music. Slightly calmer, but no less well stocked, is **Pacific Boarder** (1793 West 4th Avenue, 604-734-7245, www.pacificboarder.com).

Serious boarders also head to **Skull Skates**, formerly PD's **Hot Shop** (2868 West 4th Avenue, 604-739-7796, www.skullskates.com). One of the oldest board shops in Canada, PD's claims to have the largest selection of longboards in the country — great, apparently, for cruising the streets.

To see boarders in action, you need go no further than the plaza at Robson Square. Vancouver also hosts what's dubbed the oldest and largest (we're big on superlatives) skateboarding event in North America. The **Slam City Jam**, with a purse of $100,000 in US funds — major bucks for boarders who, it appears, live in penury — is held in early May at the Pacific Coliseum in Hastings Park. **Hastings Park** (East Vancouver) has its own outdoor skate bowl. Skullskates. com, which lists regional skate parks, describes Hastings as "(a) weird, hard to describe 'pit' (street) area, two mini-horseshoe bowls leading into snake run/half pipe, leading into ten-foot-deep bowl with two feet of vert, continuos [sic] metal coping everywhere." Another option is **Cooper's Park** (Downtown South), under the north end of the Cambie Street Bridge. The newest park is the **Vancouver Skate Plaza** under the Georgia Viaduct, near Union and Quebec streets and Expo Boulevard.

SECRET

BODYWORK

To many, BC is California North. Everything born in Valhalla eventually migrates up the coast, and Vancouver sometimes sees itself as a Californian lab for the rest of this country. No surprise, then, that all things New Age — particularly that odd and wonderful sector known as bodywork — are huge here. If you don't believe me, pick up a free copy of the monthly magazines *Common Ground* ("fitness, culture, creativity") or *Shared Vision* ("Improving the Quality of Your Life") at most health-related stores, libraries, and New Age–friendly outlets. In these publications, you'll find a dazzling array of specialists and services, ranging — and this is a big, open range — from shiatsu and meditation to ear candling (which sounds ominously like those itinerant street vendors in India who poke around your inner sanctum for accumulated wax).

On it goes: tantra and sex; bio-dentistry; lymphatic drainage; color and sound therapy; acupressure and acupuncture; sacred-circle tarot readings; and, I love this, "core-belief engineering." There's also yoga, travel, rentals, restaurants, "looking good," and lots of articles along the lines of "Iroquois Speaks Out for Mother Earth."

But back to bodywork. I can report from firsthand experience that

Hellerwork — a system of "structural integration bodywork," ideal for people with injuries or severe stress — is a helpful experience. Among its best Vancouver practitioners is Jenny Lou Linley (604-733-0339).

Naturopath **Dr. Sid Weiss** (604-877-1702, www.drsidweiss.com) practises what he calls energy medicine—therapies that foster innate healing. **Hideo Takahashi** (604-736-2430), a registered acupuncturist, comes highly recommended. **Samaya Ryane**, a proponent of Japanese-based spiritual and physical practice of Reiki, offers "a unique relaxation massage affecting body, mind and soul" (West End, 604-676-0761).

Actually, there are lots of dual-gifted reiki healers out there, some of whom also do "chakra balancing." For names and options, visit the **Reiki Alliance** at www.reikialliance.com.

For **hypnotherapy** and past-life regression, Diana Cherry (604-731-2646) comes recommended by those who've been back, and forward again.

The **Massage Therapy Centre** (158 East 11th Avenue, East Vancouver, 604-873-4150), which includes a resident Chinese medicine expert, is nicely ensconced in a heritage building just off Main Street.

S E C R E T

BOOKS

White Dwarf Books (3715 West 10th Avenue, Westside, 604-228-8223) specializes in science fiction and fantasy. **Dead Write** (4333 West 10th, Westside, 604-228-8221, www.deadwrite.com for both stores) deals in crime and detection.

Downtown, **Albion Books** (523 Richards Street, 604-662-3113) is small but packs in the modern fiction, philosophy, music, art, and, a specialty, books on chess. There are also used jazz CDs and collectible LPs.

And, if you don't mind disorganization, wade into **MacLeod's Books** (455 West Pender Street, 604-681-7654). Owner Don Stewart is one of the city's most knowledgeable secondhand and antiquarian booksellers (mind over clutter).

I'd be remiss in not pointing out **Banyen Books** (3608 West 4th Avenue, Kitsilano, 604-732-7912), the lodestar of the city's counterculture and New Age movements. It's a well-stocked source of all things health related, spiritual, and otherwise healing. (Also in the complex you'll find **Banyen Sound**, 604-737-8858).

For those whose desires run toward physical nourishment, check out **Barbara-Jo's Books to Cooks** (1740 West 2nd Avenue, Kitsilano, 604-688-6755, with satellite in the Net Loft, Granville Island, 604-684-6788, www.bookstocooks.com), both a beautifully appointed and culinarily sophisticated shop dedicated to most things delicious.

At the other end of the ideological spectrum sits **People's Co-op Bookstore** (1391 Commercial Drive, East Vancouver, 604-253-6442), a member-run business that remains doggedly supportive of local writers and social justice issues, and sells books of local history and interest.

The long-time and well-loved "progressive and radical" bookstore **Spartacus**, for many years a downtown Hastings Street institution, has gone east (684 East Hastings Street, Eastside, 604-688-6138, www.spartacusbooks.org). But it still welcomes lingerers, host forums and poetry readings, and provides books and magazines on subjects that include labor, women, politics, economics, and the Canadian-International.

For a strong collection of foreign-language books and magazines, there's **Sophia Bookstore** (450 West Hastings Street, Downtown, 604-684-0484, www.sophiabooks.com.)

Elaine Perry's **Vine & Fig Tree Books** (4109 Macdonald Street, Westside, 604-734-2109, www.vineandfig.ca) sells an intelligent mix of religious and spiritual fare.

S E C R E T

BREAKFAST

A national newspaper columnist argued recently that breakfast or brunch is an overrated social institution — putting a serious dent in your Sunday morning, and adding ill-needed pounds in the form of Belgian waffles and eggs benedict. Maybe that's why the crowds that inevitably cluster on the sidewalks outside **Sophie's Cosmic Café** (2095 West 4th Avenue, Kitsilano, 604-732-6810) and **Joe's Grill** (2061 4th Avenue, Kitsilano, 604-736-6588; also 1031 Davie Street, West End, 604-682-3683) lean to the youthful. Adding support is the fact that Joe's classic bacon and eggs plate is deemed "best comfort food" in town by the *West Ender*.

Infamous is the **Elbow Room Café** (560 Davie Street, Downtown South, 604-685-3628). This is one of those places where good-natured abuse comes with the twelve-inch pancakes and bottomless cups of coffee (guaranteed to be served with a grudge).

You can't do better for brunch (or any meal, actually) than the **Tomato Fresh Food Café** (2486 Bayswater STreet, Kitsilano, 604-874-6020). Known for its healthy produce and intelligent menu, this diner-like space has an almost cult following. A genuine retro diner with a good reputation is **The Templeton** (1087 Granville Street, Downtown, 604-685-4612). While the Big Ass breakfast is recommended for people about to run the Vancouver Marathon, the restaurant serves meals well into the evening for less ambitious types. In a budget neighborhood, funky **Slickety Jim's Chat and Chew** (2513 Main Street, East Vancouver, 604-873-6760) is home to a cheap "roadhouse breakfast" (eggs, potatoes, and toast).

The **Tomahawk Barbeque** (1550 Philip Avenue, North Vancouver, 604-988-2612, www.tomahawkrestaurant.com) has been around for decades, though not as long as the Capilano Indians of this North Shore. I remember when the Tomahawk was a rustic log cabin serving excellent hamburgers (and paper fortunes); it has long since relocated and "repositioned" itself, as they say, and is now widely known for its heady, old-fashioned breakfasts.

SECRET
BREWERIES

Dockside Brewing Co. (1253 Johnston Street, 604-685-7070) is located within the Granville Island Hotel — itself something of an overlooked location at the eastern end of Granville Island. House-brewed pilsners, lagers, and ales are served in a comfy wood-paneled lounge with bar and patio.

At 1441 Cartwright Street stands the original site of a pioneering and perennially popular BC craft brewery, **Granville Island Brewing** (604-687-2739), with tours, tasting room, and retail shop. Its long-neck bottle label became so familiar that the brewery outgrew the constraints of its landmark site at the entrance to Granville Island and now makes most of its beer in Kelowna, BC. The brewery is known for its lagers and ales, all named for nearby locations — such as Gastown Amber Ale, Kitsilano Maple Cream Ale, and Cypress Honey Lager.

Yaletown Brewing Co. (1111 Mainland Street; brew house, 604-688-0064; restaurant, 604-681-2739), sited in a former warehouse in once-industrial Yaletown, makes its brews on the premises. It then transfers them to the bar taps using an English "beer engine" and series of hand pumps. Brew house designer Frank Appleton, from the north of England, likes the emphasis on malt in Frank's Nut Brown Ale; Yaletown also makes Double Dome Stout, Harbour Light Lager, Red Brick Bitter, and Indian Arm Pale Ale.

"Beer hounds" frequently show up at **Storm Brewing Ltd.** for their "unfiltered ales" (310 Commercial Drive, East Vancouver, 604-255-9119). This is a small brewery that turns out a fine five-year-old barrel-aged cherry lambic. It also makes an Indian pale ale (Hurricane IPA), Black Plague Stout (love it), Highland Scottish Ale, and a traditional German-style Pilsner called, inexplicably, Precipitation Pilsner. Don't just turn up. This is a cottage industry with limited staff. If you're looking for brewing equipment, contact **Dan's Homebrewing Supplies** (692 East Hastings Street, Downtown Eastide, 604-251-3411, www. beermaking.ca).

SECRET

BUDDHIST

The **Buddhist Temple** (9160 Steveston Highway, Richmond, 604-274-2822, www.buddhisttemple.org), built by the International Buddhist Society, is a glitzy but genuinely spiritual temple — ideal for a day's outing to exotic realms. The temple describes itself as the most exquisite example of Chinese palatial architecture in North America. The exterior features a curvaceous roof of "golden porcelain tiles" and a stairway flanked by marble lions. The complex embraces the Main Gracious Hall and Thousand Buddha Hall, a meditative garden with a "wisdom fountain," and a stone path that leads to the "always cheerful" Maitreya Buddha. Inside, there's unending art and craftsmanship of a grandiose nature. Hey, let's be honest about this: this temple is way, way over the top.

There are other Buddhist institutions around, including the imposing if impermeable-looking **Vancouver Buddhist Church** in the troubled area of Powell Street and Oppenheimer Park (220 Jackson Street, East Vancouver, 604-253-7033). This historic neighborhood church, affiliated with the Jodo Shinshu (True Pure Land) sect based in Kyoto, as well as with the Buddhist Churches of Canada, maintains an active calendar. There's also the relatively new **Tung Lin Kok Yuen Society Temple** (2495 Victoria Drive, East Vancouver, 604-255-6337), a Hong-Kong based temple with a large activitiy program.

For a do-it-yourself at-home altar, try the **Buddha Supplies Centre** (4158 Main Street, East Vancouver, 604-873-8169). This little red-and-gold treasure house bursts at the seams with glossy ceramic Buddhas and other deities, as well as incense, joss sticks, mood-inducing lamps, and tapes.

SECRET

BUILDINGS

What's "secret" about landmark buildings, you ask? Fact is, Vancouver has never paid much attention to its architectural heritage, and even most lifelong city dwellers know little about the better examples that mercifully remain.

Vancouver has an unenviable reputation as a knock-'em-down city (a single structure, the Lions Gate Bridge, makes it into Volume 1 of Harold Kalman's *A History of Canadian Architecture* from Oxford University Press). An example of a grand building that fell to the wrecking ball was the Greek-style, neo-Classical 1917 Pantages Theatre in what is now the Downtown Eastside. However, her well-loved Spanish-baroque sibling of 1927, the 2,800-seat **Orpheum Theatre** (entrance on Smithe Street, at Seymour Street, Downtown), survives. The Orpheum boasts a large yet intimate and lusciously appointed auditorium, and lavish lobby with balconies and staircases well suited to people-watching.

The **Marine Building** (355 Burrard Street, Downtown) is a massive Art Deco affair completed in 1930 and arguably the finest structure in Vancouver. Built to celebrate maritime history — particularly the English and Spanish discoveries of the Pacific coast — it features, on its exterior, an extended frieze of decorative waves, seahorses, and marine fauna.

The lobby is equally impressive, with a terra-cotta and tile display of ships' prows and billowing sails. The marble floor and clock over the Burrard Street doorway display the signs of the zodiac in traditional design. The no-expense-spared attitude (the building was entirely and authentically restored in 1980) extends to the elevators, with ultra-ornate metal doors and interiors of mosaic wood paneling. When it was built at this prime waterfront location, one of its architects wrote romantically: "The building…suggests some great crag rising from the sea, clinging with sea flora and fauna, tinted in sea-green, touched with gold, and at night in winter a dim silhouette piercing the sea mists."

Still on the landmark theme, **Vancouver City Hall** (453 West 12th Avenue, Central Vancouver, 604-873-7011) remains a major cubic statement, dominating the central city south of the downtown peninsula. A leftist friend finds it monolithic; I like it. Really a perfect pile of hard-edged geometric blocks, the building features fine Art Deco-Moderne detailing. The interior, particularly the lobby and stairwells, is rich in stone, brass, and woodwork, lovingly applied. The Council Chambers, too, are worth investigating — a suitable blend of traditional and modern.

From the 1930s on, Vancouver architects — innovative by reason of being west of the mainstream at that time — adopted Modernism and Internationalism. The period from that point through the early 1970s is widely seen as the city's Golden Age of Architecture. Buildings generally opened up not only to the natural elements, but also to the human. Among the most celebrated structures of the period is the BC **Electric Building**, now the residential **Electra** (at Burrard Street and Nelson Street, Downtown). This twenty-two-story tower is noted for its tapered, lozenge-like appearance, and the curtain of glass that floods the interior with natural light. The scale-like decoration up the side of the building was once green and blue, the choice of artist-designer B.C. Binning.

Binning was a key figure of this period, and his home, the **B.C. Bin-**

ning House (West Vancouver), is one of a number of wood-frame, flat-roofed, open-to-nature homes on the North Shore and University Endowment Lands said to be exceptional expressions of the International Style and its regional variant, the West Coast Style. A prominent architectural writer recently chronicling the woes of the Toronto design scene wrote: "The hippest thing in Toronto design these days is Vancouver Modernism of the 1950s."

Another Modernist masterpiece is the **MacMillan-Bloedel Building** (on the northeast corner of Georgia Street and Thurlow Street, Downtown). It was designed by Canada's premier architect of recent decades, Arthur Erickson (see "Secret Arthur Erickson"). Built as headquarters for a since-dissolved BC forestry firm, this concrete giant features deeply recessed, waffle-effect windows, creating "a powerful image," writes Harold Kalman in his *History of Canadian Architecture.*

Erickson also designed the **Museum of Anthropology** at UBC (6393 Northwest Marine Drive, 604-822-5087, www.moa.ubc.ca). On a ledge overlooking Howe Sound, the MOA is formed by a series of reinforced concrete frames, or posts with crossbeams, inspired by native longhouses. The result is a spectacular space for the best of the remaining historic totem poles and other Indian artifacts.

Still at UBC, the 1992 **First Nations House of Learning** and longhouse (1985 West Mall, 604-822-8940, www.longhouse.ubc.ca) deftly combines traditional Indian structures with West Coast Modernism. The **Chan Centre for the Performing Arts** (6265 Crescent Road, 604-822-9197), something of a cylindrical vessel teetering on the edge of a rainforest, is equally popular with the public.

Returning to the more distant past: the **Europe Hotel** (Alexander Street and Powell Street, Gastown) is Vancouver's premier flatiron

structure. Another centerpiece is the **Waterfront Station** (Downtown), incorporating the 1913–15 terminus of the Canadian Pacific Railway. With its broad, columned façade, it's a successful expression of Beaux Arts Classicism.

For Vancouver basic, amble by a collection of roughly twenty-two nicely tarted-up wood-frame houses on the south side of Nelson Park, off Thurlow Street (West End). Saved by the sheer bloody-mindedness of local activists, this city-owned collection of houses, known as **Mole Hill**, functions as subsidized housing and a nice sample of what the neighborhood looked like in the early twentieth century. A few of the houses — including those at 1114 and 1120 Comox Street — have been painted their period "heritage" colors.

The **Architectural Institute of BC** now hangs its hat at the **Architecture Centre** on Victory Square (440 Cambie Street, Downtown, 604-683-8588). In the early 1900s, what was then known as Courthouse Square was the city center and hub for events such as a visit by the future King George V. It's since faced hard times, and the city is encouraging restoration and new housing. Take a walk through Victory Square — a park, really, so watch out for the sleeping bodies. At the northeast corner, you'll find a cenotaph honoring Canada's war dead. From the north, the flamboyant brick-and-ochre **Dominion Building** overlooks the square. Just east on Pender Street, at Beatty Street, stands the former *Vancouver Sun* and *Vancouver Province* newspapers building — a shapely tower, once topped by a golden globe. The two dailies are now housed in an uninspiring monolith on the waterfront.

SECRET

BURGERS

One of Vancouver's more dubious claims to fame is the **White Spot** chain of restaurants, founded in 1918 by Minnesota-born peanut vendor and baseball devotee Nat Bailey.

Many of us remember sitting in the back seat of our parents' car, a slightly sagging metal food tray extending — just — from window to window, devouring hamburgers gloopy with a tomato-mayonnaise sauce that has made the White Spot famous, and fries floating in vinegar (or ketchup).

The White Spot was sold to General Foods a while back, but the tradition lives, and may be best appreciated at the small **White Spot Triple-Os** that dot the city. They serve good breakfasts, but are known more for their excellent classic burgers with fries, milkshakes, and sodas. (Outlets include 805 Thurlow Street, Downtown, 604-609-7000; also 566 Granville Street, Downtown, 604-633-1006; and 1881 Cornwall Street, Kitsilano, 604-738-3888. Also at Science World, Central Vancouver; at General Motors Place, Downtown; and on a few of the larger BC Ferries ships.)

Hamburger Mary's (1202 Davie Street, West End, 604-687-1293), a diner with patio, has been serving classic hamburgers and chicken burgers (like the Louisiana-style chicken mozza) at this location for, well, forever. A neighbor claims it's expensive, but ten bucks for a gourmet-ish burger doesn't seem out of line. Alternatively, cross the Burrard Street Bridge and you'll find **Vera's Burger Shack** (1935 Cornwall Avenue, Kitsilano, 604-228-8372; also Dundarave Pier, West Vancouver and others, www.verasburgershack.com) among a cluster of eateries along Cornwall Avenue near Cypress Street. Vera's is celebrated for its meat, onion rings, and sinful, weight-inducing add-ons.

A lot of fuss has been made over **Moderne Burger** (2507 West Broadway, Kitsilano, 604-739-0005, www.moderneburger.com). In part, it's due to the fact that owner Peter Kokinis is a collector of diner-abilia: a neon clock from a vanished but once-popular Vancouver diner called the Aristocratic; a 1940s U-Select-It chocolate bar dispenser; two 1950s Multi-Mixer milkshake makers; and a Swami serviette dispenser that reads your fortune for a penny. The premises itself is a thing of beauty, and the burgers are exceptional, too. Everything, meat included, is fresh daily. Also takeout.

S E C R E T

CARIBBEAN

The Reef Caribbean Restaurant (4172 Main Street, East Vancouver, 604-874-5375, also 1018 Commercial Drive, East Vancouver, 604-568-5375), with a nice patio space and suitably Jamaican attitude, serves jerk, roti, curries, and dishes the likes of "mo'bay" — a frittata of three eggs with chorizo, tomato, onion, and cheddar cheese.

Popular Jamaican patties — sold singly or by the frozen dozen, in mild or hot varieties such as curry and spinach — are produced for businesses across town and available to the public at **The Patty Shop** (4019 Macdonald Street, Westside, 604-738-2144). The shop also makes chicken and veggie roti.

SECRET

CHARCUTERIES
❖

With its emphasis on charcuterie and cheeses, wines, many by the glass, and other libations, and a brick and chalkboard atmosphere, the **salt** is a popular hub (45 Blood Alley, Gastown, 604-633-1912, www.salttastingroom.com). It's deftly inserted into what was (and to some extent remains) a seedy alley on the edge of the Downtown Eastside, so venture cautiously while enjoying the cobble and low-lit backstreet ambiance. **SO.Cial at Le Magasin** is another attractive space in a more upscale setting in Gastown (332 Water Street, Gastown, 604-669-4488, www.socialatlemagasin.com). It offers charcuterie, terrines, sausages, bacons and cheese as well as conventional entrees, and a serious wine/drinks list. The sanctuary-like and ultra-fashionable **Uva Wine Bar** in the Moda Hotel (900 Seymour Street, Downtown, 604-632-9560, www.modahotel.ca) serves charcuterie and artisanal cheeses along with otherwise hard-to-find wines. **Oyama Sausage Co.** on Granville Island is where everyone goes for their luxury takeout — prosciutto, patés, party trays, etc. (Granville Island Public Market, 604-327-7407, www.oyamasausage.ca).

The bistro-like **Au Petit Chavignol** (845 East Hastings Street, East Vancouver, 604-255-4218, www.aupetitchavignol.com) delivers charcuterie and cheeses, paired with great wines (available by the glass). You will find it in the most unlikely of places, on East Hastings Street, on the edge of Strathcona. The owners, a mother and daughter, also run a next-door cheese emporium, **le amis du fromage** (604-253-4218, www.buycheese.com).

SECRET

CDs AND VINYL

Beatstreet Records, founded in 1996 as a small Kitsilano store, is now downtown and stocks 100,000 new and used records, DJ records and equipment (439 West Hastings Street, Downtown, 604-683-3344, www.beatstreet.ca).

At Highlife World Music (1317 Commercial Drive, East Vancouver, 604-251-6964, www.highlifeworld.com) the African continent is divided into regions — and artists of Abyssinia and Zanzibar, for example, are remarkably well represented. Highlife also handles sub-specialties, such as flamenco, gospel, and reggae.

Sikora's (432 West Hastings Street, Downtown, 604-685-0625, www.sikorasclasical.com) claims the largest classical collection in the city. It also stocks such a sizable collection of classic vinyl, old and new, that it routinely ships hefty packages to small but intense communities of audiophiles in the US and Asia.

For just about everything post-1950 and pop rock–related, head to spacious Zulu Records (1972 West 4th Avenue, Kitsilano, 604-738-3232, www.zulurecords.com). Stock, new and used, covers indie rock, experimental and electronic music, and strange and hard-to-get domestic and imported labels. You'll also find blues, jazz, reggae, and folk — after all, this is Kitsilano.

Neptoon Records (3561 Main Street, East Vancouver, 604-324-1229, www.neptoon.com) sells collectible LPs, 45s, posters and flyers and other memorabilia.

SECRET

CHEAP STUFF

There's a small piece of Vancouver that is once and forever hippie, and one of its meccas is **Rasta Wares** (1505 Commercial Drive, East Vancouver, 604-255-3600). Owner Patrick Iannone travels annually to Asia and South America to buy hand-knit sweaters, bamboo didgeridoos, teak drums, Thai fisherman pants, and so many styles of woolly hat you'd think the place was run by a crazed milliner. Most everything, says Iannone, is handmade of natural materials.

Two blocks north, on the opposite side of the Drive, **Beckwoman's Folk Art** (1314 Commercial Drive, East Vancouver, 604-254-8056) is spottable for its casbah-style entrance. Bonita (no surname) has run the place for twenty years, and keeps it chock-a-block with cheap clothing, jewelry, and assorted junk she buys overseas. Beaded curtains are a specialty.

Wonderbucks (909 West Broadway, Central Vancouver, 604-742-0510; and 1803 Commercial Drive, East Vancouver, 604-253-0510 www.wonderbucks.com) sells a lot of unexceptional kitchenware and garden stuff, but it's worth seeking out for its hard-to-find aluminum, tin, and wrought-iron containers and decorative fixtures, as well as gorgeous wrapping paper and fridge magnets.

Army & Navy (36 West Cordova Street, Downtown, 604-682-6644, www.armyandnavy.ca) is the department store for all things cheap, and it's looking pretty spiffy (if you don't look too closely) since millionaire socialite Jacqui Cohen accepted the challenge of keeping the family firm afloat. It's been at this location for generations ("since 1919"). The selection is wide ranging to say the least — from cheap runners, through markdown sheets and towels, to cut-price Chef Boyardee Beef Ravioli.

SECRET
CHINATOWN

Vancouver's **Chinatown** deserves a Secret book of its own — so many are the little-known sights, including well-hidden former opium rooms and a surviving underground passage that once housed bathing facilities and barber chairs.

But when I mention to a Chinese historian that I'm planning to recommend an amble down the lane behind Keefer Street to see the (since relocated) Keefer Laundry, he warns me that I'm putting visitors unaware of the downtown drug scene at risk. So stick to the main streets — and they *are* safe, even at night, in my view.

Chinatown is roughly bounded by Gore, Georgia, Abbott, and Pender streets; East Pender and Keefer are the liveliest. The powers that be suggest you enter Chinatown from the west, along West then East Pender Street, where a grand gate on the San Franciscan model has recently been erected at Taylor Street.

Eastward on Pender, particularly between Carrall and Main streets, you'll find decorative, neo-Colonial buildings. Some have porches suggestive of steamy South China, from which most early immigrants came. This area is also home to the **Chinese Cultural Centre** (50 East Pender Street, 604-658-8865) and the adjacent **Museum and Archives** (around the corner at 555 Columbia Street, 604-658-8880). Both mount exhibits; the museum has several galleries hosting often-excellent exhibits of Chinese culture and politics that tour the world.

East Pender Street is also the place for Chinese imports, from cheap baskets to expensive furniture, jade, and Oriental art. Cross Main Street, and you enter the produce, meat and fish, and restaurant district — the sidewalks are crowded and the buzz genuinely Asian.

These are reserved people, who may frown or turn away if you try to take photos. The food merchants will handle your purchase with utter indifference, even a chill: I put it down to fear or discomfort. But look beneath the cool service and you'll see a warm, smart, industrious community making the best of a far-from-easy immigrant life.

For a look back in time, quietly climb the interior stairs of the **Chung Ching Taoist Church** (on the north side of Keefer, just east of Main). In a third-story temple, where the air is thick with incense, you will see an elaborate gilded altar filled with spiritual figures and ceremonial objects. Possibly, a couple of elderly people will be there, backs bent over a newspaper.

Chinatown is justly proud of the **Dr. Sun Yat-Sen Classical Chinese Garden** (behind the cultural center at 578 Carrall Street, 604-662-3207). Though no secret, this was the first formal scholar's garden built outside China by skilled craftsmen and is worth a visit.

But for the best Chinatown experience, just walk the streets with the knowledge that this is a community that has been through a huge struggle — from the early days, when Chinese were largely excluded from white society, to ongoing battles to compete with suburban malls that serve the huge Chinese diaspora, and with the crime and drug-driven behavior that trickles down from East Hastings Street.

On summer weekends, a **Chinatown Night Market** runs on Keefer Street, between Main and Columbia. The **Chinese New Year parade**, usually held in February, has evolved into a spectacular affair.

SECRET

CHINESE FOOD

Vancouver has hundreds of Chinese eateries, ranging from the cheap and sustaining, such as **Legendary Noodle** (4191 Main Street, East Vancouver, 604-879-8758); to the traditional and expensive, such as the **Imperial Chinese Restaurant** (335 Burrard Street, Downtown, 604-688-8191, www.imperialrest.com); and including the hip, or "modern Chinese," of **Wild Rice** (117 West Pender Street, Downtown, 604-642-2882, www. wildricevancouver.com).

Actually, Wild Rice is in some outer Oriental cosmos. I mean, how do you categorize a slightly listing stack of Shanghai sweet-and-sour sticky ribs with root and tuber frites, followed by a sauté of long and glistening green beans with chilies and almond brittle, capped with grapefruit and lychee sorbet and Mandarin oolong tea? For added pleasure, watch the happenings from the terrace bar while you wait for your table (no reservations).

Back on earth, you can pick up cabbage-and-noodle dumplings, steam buns filled with beans or taro-root paste, and sweets such as pineapple spring cake at the family-run **Tachia Bakery and Deli** (4111 Macdonald Street, Westside, 604-731-7766).

For middle-of-the-road Chinese, the Cantonese-style **Hon's Wun-Tun House** is always topping someone's best Chinese list and is perennially busy. The most authentic locations are, of course, in Chinatown (280 Keefer Street, 604-688-0871, www.hons.ca), where pans flame on the open grill and everything moves at a hyper-efficient Chinese pace. But Hon's is also downtown (1339 Robson Street, 604-685-0871), where you can order heaping bowls of Hong Kong–style congee, plates of barbecued meats, and vegetarian options.

A cheap option is **Ho Ho's Kitchen** (1224 Davie Street, West End, 603-688-9896); a late-evening eatery is the **Congee Noodle House** (141 East Broadway, East Vancouver, 604-879-8221).

For those looking for a typically spacious Cantonese restaurant filled with extended families seated around a white-cloth-covered circular table, you can't go wrong with the **Pink Pearl Chinese Restaurant** (1132 East Hastings Street, East Vancouver, 604-253-4316, www.pinkpearl.com). Keep your eye on the parade of dim-sum wagons that arrive loaded with steaming goodies and return to the kitchen empty.

According to New York food writer Steven "Fat Guy" Shaw: "Vancouver is, in my experience, the best place in North America to eat Asian food, but…the action now is in Richmond — also known as Asia West — where I've had the best dim sum and seafood I've experienced outside of Asia." Chinese foodies should get over to Richmond and just roam (see "Secret Asian Malls"). I'll recommend a restaurant well along on the road to Richmond: **Red Star Seafood** (8298 Granville Street, South Vancouver, 604-261-8389).

SECRET

CHOCOLATE

❖

Rogers' Chocolates was founded in Victoria in 1885, and remains a provincial, though not widely marketed, institution. **Rogers' Chocolates Granville Island** (1571 Johnston Street, Granville Island, 778-371-7314, also at The Landing, 389 Water Street, Gastown, 604-676-3452, www.rogerschocolates.com) stocks these luscious 1.6-ounce Victoria creams in classic chocolate, orange, and vanilla, but also (flavors change) lemon, caramel rum, and orange pecan. Note: These oversized treats are commonly sliced into two or three pieces. Boxes, sold worldwide (www.rogerschocolates.com), start at $30.

Vancouver dessert, pastry and chocolate-maker Thomas Haas, has generated wave after wave — winning numerous awards, and awing palates at a former sidewalk café in the Hotel Georgia. Now he's turned his artisanal attention to a wide-ranging business (www.thomashaas.com) that includes the **Thomas Haas Patisserie and Café** (128–998 Harbourside Drive, North Vancouver, 604-924-1847). On the chocolate front you'll find a champagne truffle — "layers of chocolate, almond and hazelnut sponge between Champagne ganache." Also (among many others) a dark-chocolate "salted caramel pecan square," a milk chocolate ganache infused with green cardamom and Whiskey, and truffles made with Cognac or Jamaican rum.

It may sound bizarre, but master chocolatier Greg Hook of **Chocolate Arts** (2037 West 4th Avenue, Kitsilano, 604-739-0475) uses designs by renowned Haida carver Robert Davidson to create works of edible art. Authentic aboriginal motifs of the frog, killer whale, and eagle are molded onto high-grade bittersweet Belgian chocolate, which is filled with dried blueberries and hazelnut, and packaged in elegant boxes.

SECRET

CHURCHES

Vancouver isn't a particularly churchy city. However, early immigrants — especially Methodists, Presbyterians (most of whom joined what became the United Church of Canada), Anglicans, and Baptists — built stalwart granite structures such as the neo-Gothic **St. Andrew's-Wesley United Church** (1012 Nelson Street, Downtown, 604-683-4574) and the older and boxier **First Baptist Church** (969 Burrard Street, 604-683-8441) across the street.

You have to get well off the beaten path to see what is arguably the most impressive, or unusual, church in the city: **St. James' Anglican Church** (303 East Cordova Street, Downtown Eastside, 604-685-2532). Designed by a noted English architect in absentia, this imposing exposed-concrete structure blends Art Deco modernity with Gothic, Byzantine, and Romanesque features, both inside and out.

The **Canadian Memorial United Church and Centre for Peace** (1806 West 15th Avenue, Central Vancouver, 604-731-3101) is a modest-sized brick structure notable for its Books of Remembrance commemorating the dead of two world wars and remarkable stained-glass windows depicting pivotal events in the evolution of Canada. It's also pretty from the outside.

The Catholic Church also maintains a strong presence. Its **Holy Name Parish** (4925 Cambie Street, Central Vancouver, 604-261-9393) is architecturally stunning — an ultra-elegant tent-shaped structure with a decorative façade both ornate and intelligent. The large Filipino parish of **St. Patrick's Parish** (East Vancouver, 604-874-7818) has opened a spanking new cathedral on Main Street near its former site on East 12th Avenue — nothing over the top, but impressive indeed, given that church-building isn't too common these days.

A Catholic landmark is **St. Paul's** Gothic-Revival church on the Burrard Indian Reserve (North Vancouver). A National Historic Site, it was built by the Oblate Fathers in 1884 on the site of an earlier mission church. With its octagonal towers, pointed arch, and central rose windows, it can be spotted from around Burrard Inlet.

Three rust-colored domes and the distinctive crosses of Eastern Orthodoxy on the **Russian Orthodox Church of the Holy Resurrection** (75 East 43rd Avenue, South Vancouver, 604-325-1922) come as a bit of a shock in an otherwise ordinary, working-class neighborhood. No less of an anomaly is a small blue-and-white domed **Russian Orthodox Holy Trinity Church** (710 Campbell Avenue, Strathcona, 604-253-5562). Russians settled in Strathcona in the early and mid-1900s. The sign on the door of the church is in Cyrillic text.

A little bit of rural England, including William Morris-style windows, **St. Francis in the Wood Anglican Church** nestles into the forested landscape above Caulfeild Cove (4773 Piccadilly Street, West Vancouver, 604-922-3531). It's popular for summer weddings.

SECRET

CIGARS

Cuba thumbs its socialist nose at US foreign policy by exporting between 150 and 200 million cigars a year, mainly to Europe, but also to Asia, the Middle East — and Canada. The only reason you'll find cigar shops all over Vancouver is American visitors. They may come to Canada for this item alone, and they obviously buy — big time.

Revolucion Cigars (1062 Mainland Street, Yaletown, 604-662-4427) is a typical outfit. Here you'll find popular brands like Cohiba (a twenty-five-cigar box of Cohiba "esplendidos" goes for more than US$500 in bargain-basement Cuba — so be warned). The store also sells Monte Christo and Romeo y Julieta, each beautifully displayed in glass-fronted humidors, along with a few of the 200 other varieties produced in the factories and backrooms of old Havana. Revolucion, like all the cigar vendors, "ships" (read into this what you will). Tellingly (or not) it has recently added "men's gifts."

Several city outlets offer more, among them **La Casa del Habano** (402 Hornby Street, Downtown, 604-609-0511). Here, for a monthly membership fee, you get your own locker in which to store your bottle of high-end scotch or port, and the opportunity to hang out in a well-appointed rear lounge with like-minded aficionado. More importantly, the business claims exclusive access to Habanos premium cigars.

CINEMA

Filmgoers to the newish **Vancouver International Film Centre and Vancity Theatre** (1181 Seymour Street, Downtown, 604-685-0260; film information hotline 604-683-3456, www.vifc.org) think they've died and gone to heaven. The state-of-the-art facility, with the latest project and sound equipment, and ultra-comfortable seats and plentiful legroom in a 175-seat theater, has moved the art of the cinema, and by association the motion picture industry, a step forward. It offers year-round screening of Canadian and international films and well as support for the local film-making community.

Anyone seriously interested in the art and politics of filmmaking should get to **Pacific Cinematheque** (1131 Howe Street, Downtown, 604-688-8202, www.cinematheque.bc.ca). If, like many of us, you've let your alternative-film habit slip, this is the place to renew a rewarding relationship with offbeat, controversial, historic, or obscure domestic and foreign films. Cinematheque listings, in a free bi-monthly program, are available in most public libraries and community centers. Recent series, for example, include the work of independent Palestinian film-maker Sobhi al-Zobaidi and films on art and activism as they relate to AIDS.

A popular movie venue — very '50s-ish — is the aptly named **Hollywood Theatre** (3123 West Broadway, Kitsilano, 604-738-3211). It reruns the mainstream majors along with some alternative fare. All Monday seats are dirt cheap. Another inexpensive option, leaning more to the alternative and indie scene, is the **Ridge Theatre** (3131 Arbutus Street, Kitsilano, 604-738-6311). Lineups can run right around the leafy Arbutus Ridge block, so get there early on a weekend night. Among the Ridge's charms are a snack bar with real alternatives to popcorn dripping with oil, and a glassed-in "crying room" for babies and parents.

Another option is **Vancouver East Cinema** (2290 Commercial Drive, East Vancouver, 604-251-1313), half a block north of the Sky-Train terminus at Commercial and Grandview Highway.

Fifth Avenue Cinemas (2110 Burrard Street, Kitsilano, 604-734-7469) is a spiffy five-screen complex that shows new, trendy movies, including major foreign-language films. Or head to **Tinseltown** (88 West Pender Street, Downtown, 604-806-0799). This multi-screen cinema is on the top floor of the International Village, a major inner-city mall designed to house high-end fashion boutiques. The mall has had myriad financial and social problems and many of the storefronts are empty, but the Tinseltown complex survives. With large, comfy seats that invite slumping, this is the place to catch a low-priced matinée.

For those seeking Bollywood, there's **Raja Cinemas** (3215 Kingsway, East Vancouver, 604-436-1545; with recorded information in English).

S E C R E T

CLUBS AND CABARETS

Appearances deceive: Vancouver offers more in terms of nightlife than naysayers and outsiders believe or claim. This fact will become clearer when you go to **www.clubvibes.com** and click on Vancouver.

The site lists no fewer than twenty-one categories under nightlife — including lounges, after-hours, gay clubs and dancing, and links and more links to sources and venues.

Clubvibes.com also posts nightly events, upcoming happenings, and music and club reviews. It's a good idea to check out where you're going in advance, because these places come and go with amazing speed. Tracking down a phone number can be next to impossible: names change, clubs relocate, occasionally they burn down. And from time to time the city closes a late-night venue — usually for a few weeks at most — for some hours or liquor infraction.

To meet people and listen to live music, there's the civilized second-story **Railway Club** (579 Dunsmuir Street, Downtown, 604-681-1625, www.therailwayclub.com) in the business district. Retro-looking **Ginger Sixty-two** (1219 Granville Street, Downtown, 604-688-5494, www.ginger62.com) is a popular lounge, with both bar and sofa seating, where low-fi music makes conversation feasible.

The **Silvertone Tavern** (2733 Commercial Drive, East Vancouver, 604-877-2245) comes well recommended by a city music-scene writer for its affordable drinks and support for diverse Vancouver musical talent.

And on the better edge of the shady part of town, a nicely spruced up and gay-friendly **Lotus Sound Lounge** (455 Abbott Street, Gastown, 604-685-7777) has enjoyed a revival in recent years, though it can, it's said to feature "Vancouver's original Underground Sound."

The boutique **Moda Hotel** (900 Seymour Street, Downtown, 604-683-4251, www.salttastingroom.com) is a hot destination in its own right, but its Uva Wine Bar is currently a distinctly hip bar in which to hang out.

The hottest spot for the downtown hipster is, I'm told by a denizen,

Crush Lounge (1180 Granville Street, Downtown, 604-684-0355). Music runs through funk, soul, and jazz to R&B and more.

Richard's on Richards continues to pound out the rock (1036 Richards Street, Downtown, 604-687-6794) as one of the city's most popular and long-surviving club-cabarets.

The **Roxy Night Club** (932 Granville Street, Downtown, 604-331-7999, www.roxyvan.com) is celebrated for, among other things, bartenders who know both their clients and drinks well. **Sonar** (66 Water Street, Gastown, 604-683-6695, www.sonar.bc.ca) is best known for dance music that runs from hip-hop to trance. It speaks for itself when it says: "You won't give a f—— who's playing 'cuz it's all good."

BarNone (1222 Hamilton Street, 604-689-7000) may be best known for its battles with neighboring residents over early morning exit-ers; however, insiders of this very Yaletown haunt obviously like its atmosphere and music enough to kick up some fuss on departure.

A popular café-lounge-bar (with patio) for just hanging out is **Subeez** (891 Homer Street, Downtown, 604-687-6107, www.subeez.com).

Another popular venue is the **Au Bar** (674 Seymour Street, Downtown, 604-648-2227).

SECRET

COFFEE

Where to hang out can be a testy subject. That's because this city has served as something of a testing ground for Seattle-based Starbucks, and the inroads have been considerable — some say insidious. But there are other coffeehouses, and among the funkiest and most inviting is **Bean Around the World** (12 locations, including 4456 West 10th Avenue, Westside, 604-222-1400, www.cowboycoffee.ca). Lounge on a couch before a blazing (gas) fire with a newspaper and a longish espresso. Or take home a pound or two of — what else but? — Ethiopian sidamo or Yemeni mocha sanani.

Several **Bojangles** franchises have come and gone, but a good one remains on the north shore of False Creek (1089 Marinaside Crescent, South Vancouver, 604-683-7556). It serves light meals, is licensed, and offers mid-evening jazz.

A relatively new and much-heralded venue — both for its space and superior, even serious, coffee — is **49th Parallel** (2152 West Fourth Avenue, Kitsilano, 604-420-4901, www.49thparallelroasters.com). Sources for this roaster/importer include the Ethiopia Yergacheffe Konga Co-op and several estates in Kenya. The café also serves up-scale pastries from Thomas Haas and other artisan bakeries.

Delaney's (1105 Denman Street, West End, 604-662-3344) is a perennial favorite with West Enders. While the woodsy interior is cozy and crowded on a wintry day, the mere hint of sun draws people-scanners to its sidewalk tables. Delaney's also has several, including North Shore outlets, one in the Dundarave area (2424 Marine Drive, West Vancouver, 604-921-4466) and another in perfect, peaceable, suburban Edgemont, not far from the Grouse Mountain gondola (3099 Edgemont Boulevard, North Vancouver, 604-985-3385). If you're walking the seawall near the Granville Slopes, pick up a rich Italian brew at **Prego Coffee & Deli** (1625 Hornby Street, Downtown South, 604-605-3888).

I'd be remiss in not mentioning, again, **Joe's Café** (1150 Commercial Drive, East Vancouver, 604-255-1046), a granddaddy of coffee independents and an institution on The Drive, where left-wing angst co-exists with Latin Europe. For years, Joe, a former Portuguese bullfighter, has been satisfying all ends of the Commercial Drive candle, though it sputters and spits from time to time. Joe's also offers billiards, televised sport, and serious coffee.

For East Vancouver's Commercial Drive coffeehouses (some with liquor licenses) that cleave to their macho European roots, there's the **Abruzzo Cappuccino Bar** (1321 Commercial Drive, 604-254-2641); the **Portuguese Club of Vancouver** (1144 Commercial Drive, 604-251-2042); and the **Café Roma** (1510 Commercial Drive, 604-215-8801). The latter is filled with people in black leather jackets with one ear to the cell phone and one eye on perpetually televised European football. The Roma also serves Italian-style sandwiches and gelato.

But a favorite of the wider population is the brazenly Italian **Calabria Bar** (1745 Commercial Drive, 604-253-7017), outfitted with marble-like tables, plaster columns and statues, cheap chandeliers, and a painted ceiling that makes references to the Sistine Chapel. Here the mood is mellow and, in spite of the crowd, a classic cappuccino or gelato con espresso is usually made with grace and leisure.

Lastly on the Drive, there's **JJ Bean** (2206 Commercial Drive, 604-254-3723). On a sunny morning, you may spot half a dozen men smoking marijuana and drinking coffee at a sidewalk table. Vancouver-based JJ Bean also makes Torrefazione Coloiera coffees, sold at several other coffee outlets.

At last count, there were more than 200 **Starbucks** "outlets" in metro Vancouver; the one at 2270 4th Avenue (Kitsilano, 604-737-0477) is worth frequenting if only for its prime location.

Across the street, **Capers Courtyard Café** (2285 West 4th Avenue,

Kitsilano, 604-739-6676) is packed on a nice day, as is **Kits Coffee Co.** (2198 West 4th Avenue, Kitsilano, 604-739-0139). Both serve light food.

Another well-patronized independent is the **Blue Parrot**, strategically located overlooking the water in the northwestern corner of the Granville Island Public Market (604-688-5127).

Still in Kitsilano, the Connaught Apartments (2515 Vine Street) is an old wood-frame apartment house lovingly restored by its longtime owner. An artist, daughter of the owner, lives and works in one of the storefronts: the corner space is the easygoing coffeehouse **Higher Grounds** (2300 West Broadway, 604-733-0201).

On Main Street in East Vancouver, you'll find a couple of neighborly independents: at King Edward Avenue sits **The Grind Coffee Bar & Gallery** (4124 Main Street, 604-874-1588); nearer Broadway, **Monsoon** (2526 Main Street, 604-879-4001) is also a bistro-style restaurant and magazine shop. A local "secret" for coffee, I'm told, is **The Whip Restaurant and Gallery**, just off Main Street (209 East 6th Avenue, 604-874-4687).

Beautifully sited in one of those rare wedges where two streets coalesce, in this case Kingsway and Main, is **Gene** (2404 Main Street, East Vancouver, 604-568-5501). It's blessed with torrents of natural light, and outdoor seating (nice when the sun comes out).

SECRET

COOKING-SCHOOL DINING

At **Vancouver Community College's City Centre Campus** (250 West Pender Street, Downtown, 604-443-8300), you'll find a third-floor dining room, restaurant, cafeteria, and bakery with a variety of inexpensive foods prepared by cooks, chefs, and bakers-in-training.

There's also a licensed dining room and bakery at the **Pacific Institute of Culinary Arts** near the entrance to Granville Island at 1505 West Second Avenue. Call 604-734-4488 for lunch and dinner reservations.

The **Dubrulle International Culinary Institute** operates within the Art Institute of B.C., with sites in Burnaby, downtown Vancouver and on Granville Island (www.careercolleges.ca).

SECRET

CRYSTALS

For Crystal aficionados, the best sources are **Crystalworks Gallery** (1760 West Third Avenue, Kitsilano, 604-732-3870. www.crystalworks.ca) in a "green" concrete, steel and glass building with flattering light, and the Crystal Ark (1495 Cartwright Street, behind the Kids Market on Granville Island, 604-681-8900). This long-time mecca specializes in gems, stones and jewelry.

CYCLING
❧

Vancouver's serious cyclists may tell you that the scene 15 years ago was relatively bleak. However, since 1990, the city engineering department has added or defined 24 distinct cycling routes, covering a total of about 250 miles (400 kilometers).

And while this isn't Amsterdam, the **Vancouver Area Cycling Coalition** (www.vacc.bc.ca) says we now have a relatively bicycle-friendly city. The basic grid system makes it fairly easy to get around, says spokesperson Richard Campbell. If you get lost (and aren't enjoying the experience), you only have to look north to the mountains and you'll get your bearings — most streets run pretty much north-south and east-west.

Vancouver's bicycle routes are designed to get cyclists off the noisy, smelly, and aggressive main arterials. A current star of the show is the **Midtown/Ridgeway** route. It bisects the city, east to west, at its highest elevation, following East and West 37th Avenue for much of the way.

Routes defined as "bikeways" share low- to modest-use roadways with motor vehicles, although sometimes these routes veer onto paths or major arterials. Intersections have signals designed for cyclists' use.

However, some routes, like Midtown/Ridgeway, are also defined as greenways, meaning they're designed for pedestrians as well. Among the added amenities of a greenway are benches, fountains, mini-parks, and, in particular, eccentric public art.

For example, *Backstop: A Stage for Wordsworth*, at 37th Avenue and Cartier Street, reveals a theatrical baseball structure inspired by the poet's words: "This city now doth, like a garment, wear / The beauty of the morning; silent, bare / Ships, towers, domes, theatres, and temples lie / Open unto the fields, and to the sky."

"Pole art" installations on this greenway include an oversized garden rake (at Oak Street); multiple copies of some kind of metal parachute thing (Cambie Street) titled *Machina Metronoma*; and two giant perforated bicycle seats (at the Ontario bikeway junction). For details on the works, including their creators, go to www.city.vancouver.bc.ca and do a search for the public art registry.

This stretch of the Midtown/Ridgeway greenway intersects with the north-south **Ontario** bikeway, among the routes Campbell recommends. He also likes the **Cypress** route through the west side (incorporating winding Angus Drive in Shaughnessy); the crosstown **10th Avenue** route (in the process of becoming a bikeway); and the **Seaside** bikeway and greenway, which hugs the foreshore of the downtown peninsula, including False Creek and Stanley Park. The Seaside continues west through Kitsilano to UBC, where it connects with other bike routes.

Another nice little route, says Campbell, is **Portside**, running from east-side Lakewood Drive, along Burrard Inlet, past the grain elevators, to the Second Narrows (Ironworkers') Bridge.

The BC **Parkway** route, while rough in patches and not for the novice, pretty much parallels the Kingsway arterial southeast through Vancouver into Burnaby and through Central Park, connecting with the **Central Valley Greenway**. Campbell also recommends the municipality of Richmond's **Shell Trail**, which follows Shell Road past the Richmond Nature Park and into blueberry patches where cyclists can restore their energy in late August and early September.

A map titled *Cycling in Vancouver* is available at city hall (453 West 12th Avenue). It is also downloadable at www.city.vancouver.bc.ca (under engineering and cycling). The **Bicycle Hotline** is 604-871-6070.

Some city buses carry bikes: they include the #99 B-line along Broadway; the #135 between Simon Fraser University and Stanley Park; and #404 to the Tsawwassen ferry. Bikes can also be carried on West Vancouver–bound blue buses and the Seabus to North Vancouver.

For bike rentals, see "Secret Inline Skating." You can also pick up a modestly priced rebuilt bike at **Our Community Bikes** (3283 Main Street, East Vancouver, 604-879-2453). Run by PEDAL (Pedal Energy Development Alternatives, www.pedalpower.org), the workshop provides space, tools, and advice, and does repairs for a modest fee. It also works with Latin American farmers to create low-tech farm machinery employing used bicycle parts. Further, it's something of a hub for alternative types, and it has strong connections with other groups into sustainability and related issues.

Another full-service, non-profit bike shop is UBC's **The Bike Kitchen** (604-827-7333, www.thebikekitchen.com). You'll find it in the northeast loading bay of the Student Union Building.

You can also check out **Bikeworks**, run by an organization that recycles beverage containers, United We Can (49 East Hastings Street, Downtown, 604-688-9888). On the way to the shop, you'll pass through a seemingly chaotic warehouse in which dozens of understandably grungy-looking people are unloading and counting thousands of smelly containers they've picked from Dumpsters, bins, and ditches, and for which they'll receive the small deposit paid on purchase. This is a socio-cultural phenomenon and income-generating industry that embraces the lanes, parks, and nooks and crannies of the entire city. At Bikeworks, they repair huge, sturdy three-wheel tricycles with big wooden boxes used for big-time container collection from restaurants, hotels, and bars.

Some years back, Canadian Tire hosted a wildly popular bike race that traversed the brutal cobblestone streets of Gastown. In 1991, cycling hero Lance Armstrong was among those who showed 30,000 spectators how it's done. However, the race died shortly afterward because, say some, Canadian Tire didn't feel cycling was cutting it, image-wise.

Happily, in 2002, the race was revived by the owner of a brew pub and restaurant at the western end of Gastown. Local businesspeople were behind the project: "anything to revive interest in a tourist district that's had plenty of troubles" is the prevailing attitude. The annual **Tour de Gastown** (www.tourdegastown.com), now sponsored by the **B.C. Cancer Foundation**, has re-stoked the city's passion for rough-road cycle racing. The race runs in mid-July.

SECRET
DANCE
❖

Those interested in dance's training and performance aspects should look no further than the relatively new **Dance Centre** (677 Davie Street, Downtown, 604-606-6400, www.thedancecentre.ca). Something of a Modernist, glass-façade canopy laid on top of a century-old neo-Classical bank building, The Dance Centre is superbly sited on the northeast corner of Granville and Davie streets. For the past half century, this area has been pretty seedy, dominated by cheap rooming houses and X-rated stores. With the opening of The Dance Centre (financed by ScotiaBank), and the renovation of several nearby hotels and drinking spots, the area has acquired a new life, and is quite safe for evening entertainment and ambling.

The charitable foundation that established The Dance Centre went through years of political maneuvering to get the job done. At first, city council didn't like the bank's demand for a flashy rotating neon sign on its original site, within view of the Granville Street Bridge. Then the proposed building design — an architectural hybrid that pretty much ruins the modestly sized bank building — infuriated heritage types. Public debate went on and on. Finally, after project organizers shrewdly brought architect-god Arthur Erickson onto the design team, no one with any political savvy was able to do serious battle — and the project proceeded.

The Dance Centre supports more than thirty dance companies with the goal of "fostering excellence" in dance in British Columbia. It holds regular performances in its own studios and elsewhere around town.

You might want to look out for performances by **Ballet British Columbia** (604-732-5003). Director John Alleyne has been credited with bringing the company back from the brink in just over a decade and creating, according to *Vancouver Sun* former dance critic Michael Scott, new works of "grave and subtle beauty." Scott describes Alleyne's full-length *Orpheus* as exhibiting "meticulously finished surfaces polished to a soft gleam."

Since the 1940s, the grand ballroom on the fifteenth floor of what is today the **Fairmont Hotel Vancouver** (900 West Georgia Street, Downtown), known simply as **The Roof**, has been a dancer's heaven. In the 1950s, CBC Radio broadcast big-band music from here, and Dal Richards and his orchestra have been popular fixtures. Alas, the Hilton hotel chain eliminated the vaulted ceiling to accommodate wiring for elaborate lighting. While still spectacular, the room is now used mainly for weddings and other private events, so can be rented (ask for catering/banquet services at 604-684-3131). The Hilton is now gone, and the hotel has reverted to its original owner.

Another venerable dance venue is the **Commodore Ballroom** (868 Granville Street, Downtown, 604-739-4550). Ballroom is a misnomer; I doubt if a ball in the conventional sense of the word (or even ballroom-style dancing) has taken place here in half a century. Rather, local and imported acts — ranging from hip-hop madsters to African jazz combos — blow the roof off this cavernous second-story room. Meanwhile, the dance floor remains (one hopes) among the best in the city.

The Commodore and Roof are among the few extant members of the "historic hall" category of the BC **Entertainment Hall of Fame**, and you'll find a plaque to that effect in their vicinities. Others, like Isy's, the Cave, and the Palomar — what were called "supper clubs" — have vanished, which says something about the city's live entertainment history. Hall of Fame plaques mark their spots as well.

S E C R E T

DIVING AND SNORKELING

The pristine, protected waters of southwest BC are home, I'm told, to octopi "smart as cats and just as shy," as well as bright orange anemones and other surprising creatures. So this region has great diving (in frigid waters). The best areas are in **Howe Sound**: various spots between Atkinson Point and Whytcliffe Park, around islands such as Bowen and Gambier, and up to Porteau Cove, on the road to Squamish. Porteau boasts a sunken steam tug and World War II minesweeper.

At the other end of Burrard Inlet, two former US naval vessels were deliberately sunk for the pleasure of divers. They lie on the bed of **Indian Arm** off Belcarra Regional Park, east of Vancouver. A dozen other diving spots, most accessible only by boat, run up Indian Arm to sheer-faced Rockfish Wall and Crocker Island, near the mouth of the inlet.

Rowand's Reef Scuba Shop (1512 Duranleau Street, Granville Island, 604-669-3483, www.rowandsreef.com) sells and rents equipment, and claims to be the only free-diving (i.e., hold your breath) operation in Vancouver. It takes divers out locally and to the northern end of Vancouver Island — the number-two dive site in the world, according to a US dive magazine.

BC **Dive and Kayak Adventures** (1695 West 4th Avenue, Kitsilano, 604-732-1344, www.bcdive.com) includes a trip to the Helcket Wall off Gambier Island in Howe Sound in its program. Here, apparently, you'll find tube and cloud sponges so big you can't wrap your arms around them. **The Diving Locker** (2745 West 4th Avenue, Kitsilano, 604-736-2681, www.vancouverdivinglocker.com) also employs certified guides who take novices on local dives.

High Output Water Sports operates out of The Boardroom (1745 West 4th Avenue, Kitsilano, 604-734-7547, www.boardroomshop. com) and rents and sells a variety of water-related boards.

SECRET

EAGLES AND OTHER BIRDS

While hundreds of thousands of resident seagulls — from the common glaucous-wing variety with a big yellow bill to the black ring-billed seagull — gulp down the junk food we toss them and then reel over the waterfront in a dazzling display of joyous aggression, this region's location at the mouth of a great river allows it to support many more species.

The best place to see a concentration of songbirds, shorebirds, waterfowl, roosting owls — and, in late autumn, incredible flocks of migrating snow geese — is the **George C. Reifel Migratory Bird Sanctuary** (5191 Robertson Road, Westham Island, Delta, 604-946-6980). Comprising 890 acres at the very mouth of the tremendous Fraser River, this is not only a primary spring and autumn stopover for birds winging it in every direction, but also a rich, pristine natural setting intertwined with peaceful walking paths.

Those who take their birds where they find them can lean on the considerable resources of the **Vancouver Natural History Society** (604-737-3074, www.naturalhistory.bc.ca). The group was founded in 1918 by a Scottish botanist, John Davidson, who laid the foundations of gardening in BC. Today, a large membership hosts regular hikes and naturalist outings, including bird-watching in locations such as waterfowl-rich Boundary Bay and Queen Elizabeth Park, which is warbler territory. For super-serious birders, a Bird Alert (same phone number) reports precise sightings of rare or out-of-season species — perhaps a gaggle of oyster catchers at Spanish

Banks or an American black duck in Lost Lagoon.

Many people come to this part of the world solely to witness the largest concentration of eagles anywhere in North America, along the Squamish River near the village of **Brackendale**, north of Squamish (Highway 99 from Horseshoe Bay). Between November and January, you're assured of seeing hundreds of bald-headed eagles sitting in clusters in the towering trees on the far bank, and diving for spawning salmon in the cascading river.

If standing and gawking isn't enough, **Canadian Outback Adventures** (604-921-7250, www.canadianoutback.com) hosts a two- to three-hour float down the river, giving you an intimate view of these huge birds. The company supplies all the wet-weather gear, and winds up the event with a lunch at a nearby pub.

SECRET

EMILY CARR

While artist **Emily Carr** is long gone (1871–1945), her presence still hovers over British Columbia, not unlike the brooding skies that over-arch the totem poles, forests, and mountains of her rich output of drawings and paintings. Iconoclastic and outspoken, Carr once berated the head of this country's National Gallery for failing to buy her paintings: "If the work of an isolated little old woman on the edge of nowhere is too modern for the Canadian National Gallery it seems to me it cannot be a very progressive institution." No question that Carr was a progressive, sidestepping the other important Canadian artists of her era (the all-male Group of Seven)

to incorporate Cubism and Fauvism into her own uniquely fluid and abstract style.

Today, her works do hang in the National Gallery in Ottawa. As well, the **Vancouver Art Gallery** (750 Hornby Street, main entrance off Robson Plaza, Downtown, 604-662-4719) continuously exhibits part of a permanent Carr collection that spans her career. Many of these works deal with the pre-conquest native Indian reality and its spiritual dimension.

Other noted BC artists whose works the gallery frequently displays include Gathie Falk, Jack Shadbolt, Toni Onley, Robert Davidson, Jeff Wall, Gordon Smith, Lawren Harris, and B.C. Binning.

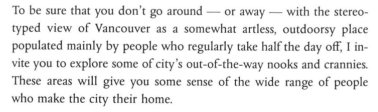

S E C R E T
ENCLAVES

To be sure that you don't go around — or away — with the stereotyped view of Vancouver as a somewhat artless, outdoorsy place populated mainly by people who regularly take half the day off, I invite you to explore some of city's out-of-the-way nooks and crannies. These areas will give you some sense of the wide range of people who make the city their home.

Shaughnessy is a somewhat understated landscape originally created by what truly old money ever existed in this city. It was named for a president of the Canadian Pacific Railway (the early financier of Vancouver), Sir Thomas Shaughnessy. Prior to World War I, the favorite architectural style was Tudor Revival. A few of these grand old mansions, interspersed with every other style from mock-Georgian to northern Spanish, can still be seen behind hedges and leafy bowers.

A good place to walk is the area just southeast of Granville Street and West 16th Avenue, beginning at the circular avenue known as **The Crescent** and continuing along **Angus Drive**, which wends westward through this ultra-affluent neighborhood. The Crescent, an oval area with five streets branching outward, is a kind of mini-arboretum, with forty-eight varieties of trees.

In the early 1970s, a family by the name of Davis began restoring an 1891 wood-frame house in the **100-block of West 10th Avenue** (near Yukon Street) in the old Mount Pleasant neighborhood, just east of city hall. So splendid and authentic was the restoration that John Davis and others went on to save other turn-of-the-century houses on the same block, tinker with the landscaping, and persuade the city to add heritage lamps. The result is a fine old-world landscape that shows Vancouver as it may (or may not) have looked at its finest moment a century ago.

The **north side of Point Grey Road** between, say, Waterloo and Alma streets is an architectural mishmash. However, if you have the good fortune to get inside one of these houses, or find your way down to the rocky beach in front, you'll experience something of Vancouver waterfront properties to die for. At the junction with Alma Street, turn north and walk a short block along the eastern edge of Jericho Beach Park and past the Hastings Mill Museum, then turn right onto **Cameron Avenue**. Cameron is less than a block long, but it's one of the city's most desirable enclaves. To complete this Kitsilano walkabout, head back west along Point Grey Road, then south on **Collingwood Street**, lined with rambling Arts-and-Crafts-style houses built in the early 1900s.

Strathcona remains a world apart. It's an idiosyncratic, working-class district built up more than a century ago by immigrant laborers — mostly Jews, Russians, and Chinese. In the 1960s, residents and political supporters of this area — east of Chinatown, and roughly bounded by Gore, Pender, Raymur, and Prior streets — defeated a city proposal to raze everything around for a network of freeways into the downtown; since then, Strathcona has mellowed into a true (and fairly politicized) neighborhood. It's notable for its unadorned workmen's houses and vegetable gardens; smallish churches and temples; humble groceries and varied parks. However, the drug-driven crime of the Downtown Eastside is never far away, which explains the heavily fortified doorways and swirling barbed wire on second-story window ledges and patios.

Southlands is a rare pastoral retreat within the city's boundaries — a horsey, garden, and hobby-farm culture in the extreme southwest of the city, south of Dunbar Street and Southwest Marine Drive, via Blenheim or Balaclava streets. Southlands Riding Club has long been a mecca for mainly female would-be equestrians, but cyclists, walkers, bird-watchers, and others seeking calm explore these country-like roads or make their way down to the north arm of the Fraser River at Deering (or Blenheim) Island.

SECRET

ENVIRONMENT

Greenpeace was founded in Vancouver in the late 1960s by a handful of mostly long-haired activist sailors bent, at the time, on halting nuclear testing by the US in the Alaskan Aleutians and by

France in Polynesia. And although the worldwide organization has had its problems over the decades, it lives on, as does Vancouver as an environmental center of sorts. Greenpeace International now runs its show from Europe, but **Greenpeace Canada**, headquartered in Toronto, remains in Vancouver (1726 Commercial Drive, East Vancouver, 604-253-7701, www.greenpeace.org).

More accessible is a store and information center operated by the **Western Canada Wilderness Committee** (227 Abbott Street, Gastown, 604-683-2567, call for hours, www.wildernesscommittee.org). While checking out the latest environmental issues and campaigns here, you can purchase books of the likes of *Fate of the Earth*, *Rainforest*, and *Camping in BC*. You can also buy books by the late, esteemed Randy Stoltmann, including his *Hiking Guide to the Big Trees of Southwestern British Columbia* and *Written by the Wind: British Columbia Wilderness Adventure*. WCWC also sells posters (most famously of whales and the Carmanah Valley), greeting cards, tree-hugger T-shirts, and handmade wooden boxes by BC artisans.

The more local **Society for Promoting Environmental Conservation** (2150 Maple Street, Kitsilano, 604-736-7732, www.spec.bc.ca) has a mandate covering everything from water quality to pesticide-free gardening. Active on the transit and cycling front is **Better Environmentally Sound Transportation** (510 West Hastings Street, Downtown, 604-669-2860, www.best.bc.ca).

SECRET

ETHNIC EATERIES
❖

A small, spirited restaurant on south Main Street that regularly makes local "best of" lists is the **Budapest Restaurant and Pastry Shop** (3250 Main Street, East Vancouver, 604-877-1949), nicely ensconced near Heritage Hall. Plan on substantial servings of goulash or schnitzel.

Another Eastern Europe (or Balkans) inspired restaurant is **Transylvania Flavour** (2120 West Broadway, Kitsilano, 604-730-0880, www.transylvaniaflavour.com). Patrons talk lovingly of the cabbage rolls—but there's much else to like, including the mamaliga, which is feta cheese and polenta balls.

A friend who lives on East Hastings Street will bus it all the way south to the Hungarian **Duna Delicatessen** (5026 Victoria Drive, East Vancouver, 604-324-2715) for their poppy-seed pastries.

And a food-writing colleague reports that one of the city's best-kept secrets is tiny Portuguese **Cinco Estrelas Restaurant** (2268 Kingsway, East Vancouver, 604-439-1124). Though dinner ends around 9 PM — Canadian- rather than Portuguese-style — this is the place, I'm told, for flambéed chorizo or pan-fried beef medallions with brandy mushroom sauce, accompanied by an Iberian wine from a limited but very satisfactory wine list.

On the west side, the simple but appealing **Kino Café**, subtitled a Flamenco Tapas Bar, (3456 Cambie Street, Central Vancouver, 604-875-1998) features sultry flamenco dancers at night who, according to a regular, "lend the whole room a sensuousness — even the windows fog up."

On the first Friday of every month, the **Ukrainian Orthodox Cathedral** (154 East 10th Avenue, Central Vancouver, 604-876-4747, www.uocvancouver.com) hosts a dinner — pierogi, borscht, and other traditional dishes — at friendly round tables in the church hall. It's a popular, welcoming event in a fine heritage building and, at last report, only 11 bucks.

The Freybe family has been making quality European sausage in Vancouver for half a century. But you can get these and other deli meats cheaply at the **Freybe Factory Outlet** (1927 East Hastings Street, East Vancouver, 604-255-6922). A budget-conscious east-sider of Ukrainian heritage, who especially likes their wine chorizo, claims that the bits and pieces sold mid-weekly as "dog food" are perfectly good for human consumption.

A secretguides.com correspondent recommends the **Round-up Café** (10449 King George Highway, Surrey, 604-581-0337). Sandwiched between a bank and a gas station near 104th Avenue, this magnet serves, I'm told, authentic pierogi dishes and awesome lemon pie.

S E C R E T

FARMERS' MARKETS
❖

Farm Folk/City Folk, a Vancouver-based collective that represents small and organic farmers around the province, reports that BC's several microclimates — from mild Vancouver Island to the dry interior plateau — coupled with an ever-growing consumer demand for homegrown specialty foods, make this one of the best regions in North America for seasonal farmers' markets (www.eatlocal.org).

The oldest and best-known Vancouver market remains the **East Vancouver Farmers' Market**. It's held each Saturday from about 9 AM to early afternoon, from mid-May until mid-October, at Victoria Drive and East 15th Avenue (604-879-3276 for this and the following two markets). Produce from the Fraser Valley, the Okanagan, Vancouver Island, and the Gulf Islands includes the organic, the eccentric (a "camembert in ash from grapevine shoots"), and freshly snipped field flowers, as well as preserves, baking, and crafts. Politics is never far from the farmers'-market scene, and the society that runs this market hasn't been too welcoming of newcomers — in part, it says, because too many markets may cause problems for struggling farmers.

However, that hasn't stopped it from opening a **West End Farmers' Market** (on the school grounds at Bidwell and Pendrell streets), also on Saturday, and the **Kitsilano Farmers' Market**, Sundays, June to October, from 10 AM to 2 PM (Kitsilano Community Centre parking lot, off 10th Avenue and Larch Street. There's even a winter market in East Vancouver (check the location and dates at www.eatlocal.ca). Experience tells me these markets can be pretty sensitive, if not purist. For example, don't dare be overheard asking, "Where are those huge strawberries I saw at Urban Fare?"

On Thursdays, May through October, in the parking lot next to the **Granville Island Public Market** (www.granvilleisland.com), you'll find a cluster of farmers selling everything from cherries and squash to fresh honey, in season. There are lots of flowers and plants, including herbs. Also superior spuds from the Pemberton Valley.

In suburban southeast Vancouver, in what was once the city's rural outskirts, you'll be delighted to come across the **Avalon Dairy** (5805 Wales Road, East Vancouver, 604-434-2434, www.avalondairy. com). This place, the oldest existing dairy farm in BC (1908), sells glass-bottled organic milk, along with eggs, cheese, yogurt, and other delicacies, in a big shed just beyond the heritage house.

SECRET
FASHION

Unspeakably elegant, boldly colored jackets — at once contemporary and drawing on West Coast indigenous traditions — are the hallmark of Canada's foremost native designer, **Dorothy Grant**. One of the many artistically gifted Haida of the Queen Charlotte Islands, Grant makes and shows her garments, blankets, and hats at a studio near East False Creek (138 West 6th Avenue, Central Vancouver, 604-681-0201, www.dorothygrant.com). For men and women.

Luxury lingerie has found a niche in this city. **Christine Designs** (www.christinevancouver.com), by silk designer Christine Morton, have graced the limbs of Gwyneth Paltrow and Elizabeth Taylor and can be found at **Diane's Lingerie & Lounge Wear** (2950 Granville Street, Central Vancouver, 604-738-5121). They're also sold at **La Jolie Madame Lingerie** (Pacific Centre, Downtown, 604-669-1831), along with the coveted work of **Patricia Fieldwalker**, whose silk signature pieces were worn by Julia Roberts in *Pretty Woman* and Glenn Close in *Fatal Attraction*.

In the dress design category, a current star is **Yumi Eto**, whose clothes have generated something of a tsunami from here to Japan and on to Europe. Ultra-sophisticated yet still cultured, demure, and sculptural, the wonderful creations of this young Vancouverite can be seen at her Yaletown studio (by appointment only, 604-689-8320, www.yumieto.com). Appointment-only status also applies to the evening wear of **Catherine Regehr**. Stars who've worn her luxurious pieces include Kim Basinger, Gillian Anderson, Anjelica Huston, and Natalie Cole, now that we're into name-dropping. Call her Kitsilano studio at 604-734-9339 (www.catherinerogehr.com).

At the funkier end of the design spectrum, check out **Dream Apparel** (311 West Cordova Street, Downtown, 604-683-7326). Owner Wendy de Kruyff stocks locally made clothes for the young and hip, including Shelley Klassen's **Blushing Designs** (read: shapely, sexy). Klassen's own **blushing boutique** (579 Richards Street, Downtown, 604-709-3485, www.blushingdesigns.com) shows off her uniquely feminine clothing. Similar lines are found at **Liquid Clothing** (2050 West 4th Avenue, Kitsilano, 604-737-1600) and **House of Jewels** (953 Nicola Street, West End, 604-662-7360).

Natural fabrics and distinctive details are the hallmark of European separates by Hajnalka Mandula. Her **Mandula Designs** are sold at shops worth seeking out in their own right. Also her own shop called **Mandula** is here (214 Abbott Street, Gastown, 604-568-9211, www.mandula.com), as well as in American cities.

Other hip, high fashion outlets include **Eugene Choo** (3683 Main Street, East Vancouver, 604-873-8874, www.eugenechoo.com); **Circle Craft Co-op** (1666 Johnston Street, Granville Island, 604-669-8021, www.circlecraft.net); and **The Block** (350 West Cordova Street, Downtown, 604-685-8885, www.theblock.ca).

I shouldn't forget FAB (2177 West 4th Avenue, Kitsilano, 604-734-0139). This very hip jeans outlet sells the likes of terry tube dresses, "hoodies," and slip-on sandals that a *Georgia Straight* fashion writer describes as John McEnroe-meets-Pamela Anderson. You get the picture.

Yet another Vancouver designer, Sara Robson Francoeur, shows her cotton, jersey, and Lycra tops, dresses, and pants at **Narcissist Design** (3659 Main Street, East Vancouver, 604-877-1555, www.narcissist. com). And not to be overlooked — if you carry a pretty thick wallet, that is — are the artfully woven, casual (if high-culture) dresses and coats of **Zonda Nellis** (2203 Granville Street, Central Vancouver, 604-736-5668, www.zondanellis.com). Her pieces can be found hanging in more than a few elegant boudoirs around the world.

Finally, **Ron et Normand** (Ron Escher and Normand Brouillette) boast Céline Dion as a client and will show off their glamorous evening wear by appointment (604-684-6244).

S E C R E T

FENG SHUI

While people have different views on and uses for this age-old art, I understand it as the manner in which a building is sited or designed — where a tree is planted or a wall built — to prevent those wily Oriental devils from getting inside and causing havoc. Practitioners say it's an ancient philosophy in which the *chi* (or "life energy") and everyday common sense unite to help us live in harmony with our natural environment. Asian house buyers take it seriously indeed. If you notice an empty house or vacant lot in a predominantly Chinese neighborhood, you can bet the *feng shui* didn't pan out.

Practitioners teach its principles for both personal and property-related uses. Businessman **Barrie Wong**, seated behind a big desk at his **Golden Jade House** in the Yaohan Centre (3700 No. 3 Road,

Richmond, 604-303-6578), knows his *feng shui*. An expert in the art of analyzing invisible energy (or *chi*), Wong predicts that the Golden Village (see Asian Malls) and Richmond will enjoy another 40 years of prosperity. "Richmond is surrounded by sea," he says. "Water represents income—money. If you have a lot of money I'd invest heavily here." For a sum, Wong will advise on various subjects.

While Edward Gutierrez, the Chinese-Portuguese owner of **Artistic Arts and Crafts** (107 East Pender Street, Chinatown, 604-682-7118), isn't a *feng shui* master, he incorporates its ideals of harmony and balance into his business. He sells jewelry — gold and jade, the latter from Burma. But you'll also find a fine collection of Buddhist statues (from obese Chinese to ascetic-esoteric Indian), healing stones, and crystals, all of which relate to energy in its positive forms, says the gentle-mannered Gutierrez. If the vibes are right (take care with this), you might quietly approach him about a Chinese reading.

SECRET

FERRIES

Some of the better tourist attractions in this city are, to my mind, the diminutive passenger ferries that variously flit and bob around False Creek, connecting the downtown peninsula with Granville Island and other points. The routes are divvied up between the original **False Creek Ferries** (Granville Island Ferries Ltd., 604-684-7781) and **Aquabus** (604-689-5858).

False Creek Ferries — with the more picturesque and exposed (and, therefore, potentially choppier and more exciting) routes — connects the Aquatic Centre near Sunset Beach with Vanier Park, Granville Island (the westernmost dock), Stamps Landing, and Science World. Aquabus sticks to the more peaceable waters between the foot of either Hornby Street or Davie Street (in Yaletown) and the Arts Club Theatre dock on Granville Island, as well as Stamps Landing and Science World. The latter also operates a bike- and carriage-carrying vessel between Hornby and Granville Islands.

Moving up the ferry ladder, there's the **Seabus**, part of the region's publicly operated transit system. It carries foot passengers, wheelchair users, and cyclists between Waterfront Station at the northern end of Granville Street and Lonsdale Quay in North Vancouver. The twelve-minute ride isn't much, though it may provide a duck's-eye view of looming freighters or cruise ships, and pretty good vistas of Burrard Inlet. Lonsdale Quay, a pseudo-farmers' market with shops, food stalls, and dockside seating, is as good a place as any to while away a sunny afternoon.

From here we jump to the forty-two-vessel BC **Ferries** fleet (www. bcferries.com). Among the smallest is the twenty-four-car **Albion Ferry**, which crosses the Fraser River between Maple Ridge on the north bank and Fort Langley on the south every fifteen minutes. Getting there requires a bit of a drive, out the Barnet Highway or Lougheed Highway (highways 7A and 7, respectively), or Highway 1.

For a Howe Sound ferry experience, ride the public West Vancouver Blue Bus from downtown Georgia Street out to Horseshoe Bay (or drive the Upper Levels Highway) and catch a car ferry to Snug Cove on nearby **Bowen Island**. Alternatively, take a slightly larger vessel to **Langdale** near Gibson's Landing, a charming village that marks the beginning of the Sunshine Coast. From Langdale, you can hop another ferry to **Gambier Island** and **Keats Island**, both speckled with summer cottages and rock-perched houses.

Or head south from Vancouver on Highway 99 to the terminal at **Tsawwassen** (city buses go that way), and ride the ferry across Georgia Strait to Galiano, Mayne, Pender, or Salt Spring island. Each island has its own distinctive character and is worth a visit.

Serious ferry-riders will want to experience one of BC Ferries' new Super C-class vessels — and the ninety-minute to two-hour ride to Vancouver Island. The one to **Schwartz Bay** and, ultimately, Victoria, leaves from Tsawwassen; a commuter bus from city to city runs from Vancouver's Pacific Central Station (1150 Station Street). Ferries and buses to **Nanaimo** depart from both Tsawwassen and Horseshoe Bay.

For schedules and fares, call 1-888-223-3779; from out of province, 250-386-3431. If you're traveling on a major route by vehicle, or pulling a boat or trailer, it's best to reserve space at 1-888-724-5223. For more information, go to www.bcferries.ca.

SECRET

FESTIVALS
❖

People who like to party en masse complain that Vancouver's a no-fun city (those who prefer more discreet affairs may disagree). But there are lots of festivals, the most visually interesting of which are organized by the **Public Dreams Society** (604-879-8611, www.publicdreams.org). Their signature event, **Illuminares**, happens in late July — a steamy, nighttime family parade of towering stilt puppets and exotic, mostly homemade, paper lanterns that wends its way around Trout Lake (East Vancouver).

Three hundred volunteers make Illuminares happen. It's so spectacular that even though organizers eschew promotion, thousands of people show up from across the region. This is also politicized Vancouver at its most egalitarian. There must be no barrier between audience and performer — we're all one here.

The society also hosts the Halloween-related **Parade of Lost Souls** in and around Grandview Park on Commercial Drive (East Vancouver).

The **Vancouver International Children's Festival** in late May and early June in Vanier Park (Kitsilano) is an incredible affair, attracting the likes of Vietnamese water puppeteers, brilliant Quebec comedians, and flying Dutch skateboarders. It spills over onto Granville Island with, for example, juggling workshops (the ideal career path for your kids, eh?). For details, go to www.vancouverchildrensfestival.com. For tickets, call 604-280-4444 after late March (www.childrensfestival.ca).

In late June, the **Vancouver International Jazz Festival** takes place at roughly 40 venues around the city — clubs, theaters, breweries, ballrooms, and public plazas. The artists and music run — in every sense — from A (perhaps the Eivind Aarset Trio of the Norwegian jazz underground) to z (Zubot and Dawson, a duo of hot Canadian acoustic musicians). For information, contact the Coastal Jazz and Blues Society (604-872-5200, www.coastaljazz.ca).

The city hops during the July–August **Vancouver International Comedy Festival** (604-683-0883, www.comedyfest.com). This is when Vancouverites' somewhat lame North American humor gets a major infusion of irony from visiting Brits and other overseas comics. It's pure joy to sit in the Market Courtyard and watch a couple of English, Scottish, or Irish rogues — with their deft manipulation

and black jokes (always at our expense) — wreak utter confusion on an otherwise rapt and delighted audience. At Triangle Square, south of the market, jugglers and contortionists attract huge crowds, and extract or extort impressive sums from them.

The **Vancouver International Wooden Boat Festival** happens annually in late August (Granville Island, 604-519-7400, www.vancouverwoodenboat.ca). Beautiful wooden boats of all types and sizes — some still under construction — float or sit around the island. The dramatic **Rio Tinto Alcan Dragon Boat Festival** is held near the end of June at the eastern end of False Creek (Downtown South, www.dragonboatbc.ca). The **Vancouver International Fringe Festival** (604-257-0350, www.vancouverfringe.com), an alternative theater event, happens on the island in September. And the ever-popular **Vancouver International Writers Festival** (1398 Cartwright Street, Granville Island, 604-681-6330, www.writersfest.bc.ca) takes place in late October.

The Vancouver Folk Music Festival trucks on every mid-July (Jericho Beach Park, Westside, 604-602-9798, www.thefestival.bc.ca). Bring a blanket, umbrella, and granola-fueled attitude for an all-round gorgeous summer event, now more than a quarter century old.

Still for music lovers, there's **Festival Vancouver** (www.festival vancouver.bc.ca) in August. It features dozens of performances of orchestral, choral, chamber, jazz, and world music at the Chan Centre for the Performing Arts and First Nations Longhouse, both at UBC, and Holy Rosary Cathedral (Downtown).

In recent years, the **Vancouver Recital Society** (604-602-0363, www.vanrecital.com) has hit musical stratosphere status under founding artistic director Leila Getz. Renowned for "discovering" young classical and avant-garde talent, her concert series routinely sell out.

Asked how she and her team do it, she says: "Sheer hard work. Tapes, videos, going to live concerts whenever we can — and keeping our ears to the ground." While the concerts run at several venues, I recommend the Chan Centre at UBC. This gorgeous, acoustically superior space is a rewarding experience in its own right. Coupled with great music, it can be awesome.

Autumn to spring, the **Friends of Chamber Music** group (604-437-5747) brings in big-name trios, quartets, ensembles, and small orchestras for concerts, usually held at the Vancouver Playhouse (Downtown).

Back to jazz and blues, the **Burnaby Blues & Roots Festival** happens at Deer Lake on a Sunday in August (604-291-6864, www.burnabybluesfestival.com).

SECRET

FINN SLOUGH

This place is a paradox. On one hand, squatter residents (entitled to the land or not, depending on your viewpoint) don't really fancy a lot of people wandering the creaky boardwalks that make this marshy island near the mouth of the Fraser River habitable. On the other hand, they're anxious to promote their efforts to save the history and ecology of this particularly pristine pocket of the Fraser River basin. So they've posted a Web site (www.finnslough.com) that tells the unusual **Finn Slough** story and includes a map.

There, you can read about an absentee landowner who's trying to reclaim the island and surrounding habitat for conventional development, and the political and legal efforts of residents and supporters to keep this undisturbed wetland, filled with wildlife, just as it is. Named for Finnish fishermen who settled here in the 1880s, and occupied over the years by fishers of various backgrounds, Finn Slough remains a beguiling tumbledown settlement in an unspeakably beautiful setting. Depending on the tides and seasons, you'll see fishing boats listing in the estuary mud, bobbing among the old wharves and river reeds, or being repaired in the sheds along the dike.

To get there, take Highway 99 to Richmond, and travel all the way south on No. 4 Road until you reach the river. Cross a wooden footbridge, and (unless the tide has played havoc with this Louisiana-style bayou) you'll find yourself quietly ambling among wooden shacks. Some are floating houses, others are built on scows or stilts; most are decorated with humble and playful fixtures, artifacts of river industries, and plants and flowers.

SECRET

FOODIES

Anyone interested in the serious arts of eating and drinking can get the inside scoop from the Web site **www.planitbc.com**. This is the creation of an enterprising woman who gave up marketing wine to keep the mutually enamored food and wine industries apprised of the latest events in town and beyond (Whistler is another indulgers' paradise). She now covers the entire province.

At planitbc.com, Wendy Taylor lists upcoming wine and spirit fairs, paired dinners (such as a "rosé wine and crab" event), and evenings planned around, say, food and jazz. She provides the venue and the phone number for tickets or reservations.

She also lists wine clubs and profiles top shefs.

The **Vancouver American Wine Society** (604-469-6520) brings in fabulous wines and vintners from California, Oregon, and Washington. It offers great opportunities to compare coastal wines with our own exceptional BC fare (to which I remain tirelessly devoted). People who want to carefully consider wines from south of the equator — Australia, New Zealand, Chile, Argentina, and South Africa — might consider the **South World Wine Society** (www. southworldwine.com). Through this group, you'll find information about upcoming tastings and links to yet more wine sites that will swirl you, Alice-like, into a southern hemisphere of all things grape.

There is also contact information for a **German Wine Club** and **Australian Wine Appreciation Society**. A number of Vancouver restaurants have been singled out for their wine lists. They include: **C Restaurant** (1600 Howe Street, Downtown South, 604-681-1164, www.crestaurant.com) is beautifully sited on the north side of False Creek, with views of Granville Island and the Art Deco Burrard Street Bridge. Here, you will find unabashed luxury — exceptional seafood accompanied by truly relaxed yet informative wine service. A *Los Angeles Times* travel editor I knew was so charmed by this restaurant — and its evocation of the best of the Pacific Northwest — that she quit her job and moved to Seattle (as close to Canada, one assumes, as she could get).

CinCin Ristorante & Bar (1154 Robson Street, Downtown, 604-688-7338, www.cincin.net) is beloved of the legions of diners drawn to Mediterranean cuisine, with a menu that includes alder-grilled steak, but also pizza with prosciutto. A cellar holds hundreds of wines at reasonable prices. **La Terrazza** (1088 Cambie Street, Yaletown,

604-899-4449, www.laterrazza.ca) is an oh-so-European setting of terrace dining and modern Italian food and wines.

Piccolo Mondo Ristorante, just off Robson Street (850 Thurlow Street, Downtown, 604-688-1633), is an elegant and slightly more formal Italian restaurant that serves excellent food but is particularly celebrated for its wine list (here's your opportunity to splurge big time on a special vintage).

Finally, **Raincity Grill** overlooking English Bay (1193 Denman Street, West End, 604-685-7337) brings you back to British Columbia with dishes employing local seasonal fare paired with exceptional Pacific Northwest wines (many by the glass). I love this place, but I can't forget the whole raw red onion with something stuck in it, like a cockeyed hairpin. Heck, all these guys get carried away from time to time.

Other (of numerous restaurants) singled out for their wines, if not food and ambiance, include **Cru** (1459 West Broadway, Central Vancouver, 604-677-4111, www.cru.ca); **Nu** (1661 Granville Street, Downtown South, 604-646-4668, www.whatisnu.com); and **West** (2881 Granville Street, Central Vancouver, 604-738-8938, www. westrestaurant.com).

Another source of culinary information is the excellent quarterly *CityFood* (www.cityfood.com), free at numerous outlets.

SECRET

FOOTWEAR

John Fluevog is a Vancouver success story, with foreign outlets that include Chicago, New York, San Francisco, and Melbourne. You can see what the fuss is about at **John Fluevog Boots & Shoes** (837 Granville Street, Downtown, 604-688-2828; also 65 Water Street, Gastown, 604-688-6228, www.fluevog.com). For those drawn to Betty Boop–style clunkers or Cinderella-like flights of fancy, this is shoe heaven. Fluevog makes and sells high, low, and mid-calf boots that include the Ultra Vog Grand National lace-up and the Swordfish Engineer Boot, all the better to run your enemy through with. There are also ultra-pointy Japanese slip-ons, and chunky styles that hint at Copenhagen or maybe Berlin punk. So renowned is this footwear that wearers, said to include Madonna and Marilyn Manson, are known as "Fluevogers."

Less outrageous casuals for younger feet, by trendy lines like Frye and Camper, are available at **Bionic Footwear** (1072 Mainland Street, Yaletown, 604-685-9696, www.bionicfootwear.com).

Bin lookin' for a pair of red leather, gold-studded, mid-calf boots with four-inch stiletto heels? Well, there they are at **Kalena's** (1526 Commercial Drive, East Vancouver, 604-255-3727, www.kalenashoes.com), along with other Italian shoes and boots for ladies made by Podium, Baldan, Piampiani, and others. Styles run from *très* European walking shoes to sexy dress sandals, with glitzy purses to match. Kalena's also sells similarly handcrafted footwear for men from Mauri, Vittorio Virgili, and Maros — for those who know their shoemakers.

Another outlet for hip and gorgeous footwear for any gender, with many imported lines from Argila (Spain) to Zeha (Berlin), is **umeboshi shoes** (3638 Main Street, East Vancouver, 604-909-8225, www.umeboshishoes.com).

The **Australian Boot Company** (1968 West 4th Avenue, Kitsilano, 604-738-2668, www.australianboot.com) sells tough, handsome, lace-free ankle boots made by Down Under's Blundstone Footwear (since 1870).

Finally, there's the Vancouver-born **Dayton Boot Company** (2250 East Hastings Street, East Vancouver, 604-253-6671, www.daytonboots.com). Founded in 1946 to make boots for loggers, it has since expanded into a provider of high-quality cowhide "service footwear" to ranchers, oil-rig workers, longshoremen, police officers, firefighters, and motorcyclists. It also serves the glitterati: Kurt Russell, Angelina Jolie, Kevin Costner, and Cindy Crawford are all Dayton owners. The business has even opened an outlet for its handmade footwear on LA's Melrose Avenue.

SECRET

FRANCOPHONE

In decades past, Vancouver's French-speaking community lived and did business in the neighborhood around Heather Street and West 16th Avenue. Some institutions remain, including a bilingual school and a grocery with a French name. However, much of the francophone action has shifted to West 7th Avenue, just west of Granville Street. The focal point is the **Centre Culturel Francophone de Vancouver** (1551 West 7th Avenue, Central

Vancouver, 604-736-9806, www.lecentreculturel.com). Apart from working on behalf of French-speaking Canadians (and others) who've gravitated to the coast, the center organizes events such as the annual, week-long **Festival d'été francophone de Vancouver** in late June — a series of music events around the city and a beer garden, with music, that closes this single block of West 7th to regular traffic. It's a lively affair, and everyone is welcome. In the same complex is the **Théâtre la Seizième** and **Café Salade de Fruits** (see "Secret Bistros").

S E C R E T

FROUFROU

"What wacky color," chortled a friend as we walked into the decidedly upscale and idiosyncratic "decorative homewear" shop **Peridot**, just off South Granville Street (1512 West 14th Avenue, Central Vancouver, 604-736-4499, www.peridot.ca). A mezzanine displays luxury tidbits for a tiny, would-be princess or prodigy ballerina — from delicate fairy outfits to a mauve satin-brocade blanket. The equivalent for adult girls is found in the airy downstairs gallery. Owner Tamara Wouters buys much of her stock in Paris. Intoxicating.

Also on the outer reaches of femininity is the **Barefoot Contessa** (3715 Main Street, East Vancouver, 604-879-1137), filled with similarly delightful but less expensive frippery.

GALLERIES

Long a nurturer of what is known as "cultural studies" (as in social politics) in British Columbia, what was once the UBC Fine Arts Gallery is now the **Morris and Helen Belkin Art Gallery**. It's ensconced in a suitably minimalist building on campus, flooded with natural light (1825 Main Mall, UBC, 604-822-2759, www.belkin.ubc.ca). Long under the direction of Scott Watson, the gallery shows — as it should — contemporary and often controversial work. Over the years, it has acquired the third-largest art collection in the province. It's especially renowned for representing the avant-garde artists of the envelope-pushing '60s and '70s.

The former Belkin Satellite is now the **Or Gallery** (555 Hamilton Street, Downtown, 604-683-7395, www.orgallery.org), where emerging artists show their work in a deep street-level space next to the tiny, politicized Delmar Hotel (see "Secret Lodging").

The privately run **Contemporary Art Gallery** recently moved into an award-winning concrete-and-wood building (555 Nelson Street, Downtown, 604-681-2700, www.contemporaryartgallery.ca), the better to exhibit cutting-edge artists and traveling shows from BC and beyond. It also mounts sidewalk vitrine exhibits in the windows on Nelson Street.

For somewhat more mainstream Canadian contemporary art, visit the long-established **Bau-Xi** (3045 Granville Street, Central Vancouver, 604-733-7011) or the **Equinox** (2321 Granville Street, Central Vancouver, 604-736-2405). Indeed, the entire ten blocks of Granville Street between West 16th and West 6th avenues (including the 1500

block of West 6th) is well endowed with private galleries of every ilk.

For the record, this stretch of Granville was recently redubbed **South Granville *Rise*** to better distinguish what has become a successful upscale shopping and gallery district from downtown's Granville Slopes, Downtown South, and truly South Granville (street) at the southernmost end of this major thoroughfare.

Centre A is also known as the **Vancouver International Centre for Contemporary Asian Art** (2 West Hastings Street, Downtown, 604-683-8326) and will cleanse from the cobwebbed corners of the mind any lingering preconceptions about Asian art and artists. Test this thesis by going on to the **Vancouver Chinese Art Gallery** (27 East Pender Street, Chinatown, 604-688-6848, www.centrea.org) where "contemporary" and "traditional" remain pretty much the same thing.

If you're heading to Granville Island along Second Avenue from the west, you'll pass a sheet of falling water that fronts several art galleries in the **Waterfall Building** (1540 West 2nd Avenue, Central Vancouver). The building was designed by architect Nick Milkovich with input and, importantly, name recognition from senior city architect Arthur Erickson (see "Secret Arthur Erickson"); the design took a 2002 Architectural Institute of BC medal. Frankly, I've never understood why Erickson in particular, and other designers and sculptors, are so enamored of falling water in a city where it rains nine months of the year — but what do I know (except that I get wet)? This entire area, zoned light industrial, is acquiring a cultural dimension as workshops, galleries and fashionable condos replace old-school businesses. Among recent additions is the **Edzerza Gallery** (1536 West 2nd Avenue, Central Vancouver, 604-731-4874, www.edzerzagallery. com) for traditional and contemporary works by first nations artists.

Also in this part of town is the **Diane Farris Gallery** (1590 West 7th Avenue, Central Vancouver, 604-737-2629, www.dianefarris gallery. com). It's still going strong as a representative of the avant-garde.

If you're taking in a show at the **Queen Elizabeth Theatre** (Hamilton Street, at Georgia Street, Downtown), check out the art exhibits on the mezzanine level. It's here that Civic Theatres shows the works of lesser-known or emerging artists, often on themes related to performances.

For something completely different, check out the **Gallery Gachet** (88 East Cordova Street, Gastown, 604-687-2468, www.gachet.org). The Gachet mounts strong shows on alternative and political themes in a funky space.

S E C R E T

GARDENS

I hesitate to mention **Arthur Erickson**'s house and garden on a quiet street in West Point Grey (in Westside) only because it can be devilishly hard to get into. However, there are organized tours, April through October (Arthur Erickson House and Garden Foundation, 604-738-4195, www.ericksongarden.org), so give it a try. Erickson is something of an institution on the West Coast (see "Secret Arthur Erickson"). Yet his private life has been tumultuous (to say the least) and, when he couldn't handle what must have been a considerable income, he was forced to give up ownership of his longtime home to a foundation. This home is, in reality, a garage-turned-studio cottage set in an exquisite native and Asian garden. It's a truly beautiful haven, with thickets of long grasses and bamboo, salal and huckleberry, rare Himalayan rhododendrons and a persimmon tree — entirely fenced in cedar. Hugely recommended if you like this kind of thing.

No secret, but so refined as to be routinely overlooked, is the **Nitobe Memorial Garden** (1903 West Mall, UBC, 604-822-9666, www.nitobe.org). Named for a Japanese educator who tried to bridge the gap between East and West, it is considered among the most authentic Japanese gardens outside that country. Although not large, it has a spacious feel. Gravel or evergreen-needle pathways lead you around a large, shapely pond stocked with colorful carp. A traditional bridge and iris garden bisect the waterway, and off to one side sits a traditional teahouse, used occasionally for formal tea ceremonies. But the glory here is in the trees and plants, chosen and placed to complement each other with the changing seasons and meticulously maintained. UBC also boasts a large **Botanical Garden** (6804 Southwest Marine Drive, 604-822-9666, www.ubcbotanicalgarden.org) with a garden pavilion and gift shop. Temperate, exotic, and rare plants that thrive in a coastal forest setting are its specialty, along with 400 species of rhododendron. The garden manages a total of 17 acres, including an Asian garden, sixteenth-century physic garden, and native (indigenous plant) garden, as well as the Nitobe.

The garden recently added the **Greenheart Canopy Walkway**, one of few of its kind in North America. Instead of using fasteners that damage trees, the walkway is secured by a system of interlaced steel cables designed to expand and allow for normal tree growth. The 1,000-foot walkway delivers a "bird's eye" view of a true coastal rainforest canopy. It's open, and offers guided tours, year-round (www.ubcbotanticalgarden.org and to Greenheart Canopy Walkway).

In another realm entirely are the eight disparate community gardens owned by the **City of Vancouver** — leftover tracts of land of various sizes and configurations, used by the public with conditions. These include unrestricted public access; the right to grow only flowers and food for personal use; and a community education component.

Among the oldest and most successful is the **Arbutus Rail Garden** along the old CPR and BC Hydro right-of-way. It's closely associated with the adjacent Society for Promoting Environmental Conservation (2150 Maple Street, Kitsilano, 604-736-7732).

Between Chinatown and the False Creek Flats you'll find the more spacious **Strathcona Community Garden** (off Prior Street, near Hawks Avenue, East Vancouver, www.strathconacommunitygarden. com). Here are small garden plots, a pond, a solar demonstration hut, and several orchards, including one devoted to espalier gardening. There are also lots of native plants, shrubs, and trees such as red elderberry, black cottonwood, indigenous yew, Red Oisier dogwood, and Nootka rose — more than 100 native species in all.

This garden's offshoot is the nearby **Cottonwood Community Gardens** (access at the foot of Raymur Avenue, East Vancouver). Strathcona Community Garden was created after a plan to bulldoze the surrounding area for freeways was defeated in the 1960s. And when Strathcona was taken on by veterans of that battle, Cottonwood was carved from the remaining, even less nurturing, abandoned sand bed.

Looking around Cottonwood recently, I ran into one of its founding squatters, Oliver Kellhammer, who was visiting the garden from his Cortes Island home. We walked through a section run by the Environmental Youth Alliance, and an Asian garden with persimmon, bamboo, mulberry, and Chinese chestnut.

Longtime gardener Len Kydd, who was tending his plants, sees

Cottonwood as pretty much a matter of making peace with the weeds. There's also the politics, Kydd added. "We don't argue about what goes on in the garden, we argue about the politics that impinge on the garden — like the sex trade and needle trade in the wider community. That happens here, too."

Kydd claims that Cottonwood is politically more anarchic than Strathcona Garden. Added Kellhammer proudly of Cottonwood's evolution, "It happened completely outside the bureaucratic format, without any city involvement — except benign neglect."

A remarkable wooded garden landscape is found near the Beach Avenue entrance to Stanley Park and the **Vancouver Board of Parks and Recreation** office — itself a fine 1962 example of West Coast Style (2099 Beach Avenue, Stanley Park, 604-257-8400, www.vancouver.ca/parks).

Espaliered across a granite face of the building is an Atlantic cedar tree (*cedrus atlantica glauca*, according to former parks board spokeswoman Terri Clark), meticulously tended to maintain its dramatic shape.

The surrounding woodlands, encompassing the tennis courts and pitch-and-putt course, nurture an exceptional collection of hybrid azaleas and rhododendrons relocated here in the late 1960s from a Vancouver Island nursery. Says Clark of this entirely public expanse: "These gardens and surrounding trees and shrubs are at their finest between the middle of April and the end of May. Trees — including beeches, magnolias, dogwoods, cherries, and plums — add a pink-and-white haze and soft scents to this secret refuge."

Stanley Park has other noted gardens, not the least of which is the **Rose Garden** off Pipeline Road. A small memorial garden — suitably secreted from the busiest byways — is the **Air Force Garden**

of Remembrance behind the Stanley Park Dining Pavilion. This is a natural rock garden with a pond, stepping stones, and seating, all under an arbor of trees.

Another lesser-known gem of a garden follows the public walkway just south of Granville Island, **Sutcliffe Park**, and the False Creek Community Centre. Here, a couple of parks board gardeners have gone way out of the box to produce a dense and glorious display of colors, tones, and textures that last year round.

Given that the best gardens are places where people can discover out-of-the-way niches and overlooked treasures, two well-publicized destinations merit attention. The **Dr. Sun Yat-Sen Classical Chinese Garden** (578 Carrall Street, Chinatown, 604-689-7133, www.vancouverchinesegarden.com) can be visited for its buildings alone — the hand-fired roof tiles, carved woodwork, lattice windows, and pebbled courtyard each deserve attention. But the plantings of pine, bamboo, and winter-blooming plum are said to be both "friends of winter" and expressions of Chinese virtues (which you'll learn about when you visit).

The **VanDusen Botanical Garden** (5251 Oak Street, Central Vancouver, 604-878-9274, www.vancouver.ca/parks), also open year round, is 55 acres of flowering trees, perennials, and evergreen shrubs in a well-designed setting of tranquil water features and mountain views.

Queen Elizabeth Park (West 33rd Avenue, at Cambie Street, Central Vancouver), named for the late Queen Mother (who visited Vancouver in 1939 with the newly crowned George VI), is the highest point in the city of Vancouver, at 492 feet. Here, two stone quarries have been transformed into ornamental gardens, including one devoted to roses. At the top of the 130-acre park sits the **Bloedel Floral**

Conservatory (604-257-8584), a steamy dome supporting 500 species of tropical plants and 50 kinds of exotic birds.

SECRET

GAY AND LESBIAN

You won't go wrong by starting with **Little Sister's Book and Art Emporium** (1238 Davie Street, West End, 604-669-1753, www. littlesistersbookstore.com), Davie Street being a commercial and historic hub of the city's sizable gay community. In the 1980s, Little Sister's founder Janine Fuller launched an anti-censorship battle that culminated in 2000 in a six-to-three ruling by the Supreme Court of Canada favoring Little Sister's. The court placed the onus on Canada Customs to prove that reading material is obscene before refusing it entry into the country. For documents and details on the lengthy saga, go to www.littlesisters.ca.

Little Sister's is also a mini-department store with a strong book and periodicals section, cards, videos, T-shirts, bumper stickers, leather, and whatever. It sells tickets for gay harbor cruises, plays, music (including concerts by noted gay choirs), and the events of Vancouver **Pride Week** (www.vanpride.bc.ca) and the Queer Film Festival, both held in early August and culminating in a major parade.

Like similar events across the continent, the parade draws as many as 200,000 watchers. A few snapshots: I remember a weary Bo-Peep and her companion lamb limping home on the seawall, and scantily clad sailors packing up the sound system on a flatbed truck. Little Sister's employee Mark Macdonald recalls the elderly West End gals who liked to hang from their apartment balconies and cheer on the craziness.

The **Gay & Lesbian Centre** (1170 Bute Street, West End, 604-684-5307) is the place to meet people and get involved in the local gay scene, Macdonald says. Here you'll find listings of events and team sports that range from slow-pitch softball to water polo. You can also refer to the brochure *Little Sister's Guide to Vancouver* for dozens of bars, eateries, pool halls, galleries, and saunas that particularly support a gay clientele.

The upstairs **Oasis** (1240 Thurlow Street, West End, 604-685-1724, www.theoasispub.com) is a nicely appointed pub and lounge and restaurant, with great al fresco dining. Other popular pubs with food include the spacious indoor-outdoor **Fountainhead Pub** (1025 Davie Street, West End, 604-687-2222, www.thefountainheadpub.com) and **Pumpjack** (1167 Davie Street, West End, 604-685-3417, www.pumpjackpub.com).

For disco dancing and drag, it's **Numbers** (1042 Davie Street, West End, 604-685-4077, www.numbers.ca). For candlelit dining in an "early bordello" room of velvet banquettes and Art Deco wall sconces, head to the one and only **Delilah's** (1739 Comox Street, West End, 604-687-3424, www.delilahs.ca).

At the racier end of the gay-life spectrum — definitely "fringe," says Macdonald — check out **Mack's Leathers** (1043 Granville Street, Downtown, 604-688-6225), which also does body piercing.

Gay-friendly accommodation includes **Nelson House** (977 Broughton Street, West End, 604-684-9793, www.downtownbedandbreakfast.com) and the **West End Guest House** (1362 Haro Street, 604-681-2889, www.xtra.ca).

Little Sister's publishes an annual *Gay & Lesbian Business Association*

Directory (www.glba.org). For really up-to-date happenings, pick up a copy of *Xtra West*, the community's weekly newspaper.

S E C R E T
GELATO

Of course, Vancouver loves its conventional ice cream, and you can find excellent examples at several chocolate and ice cream shops along Robson Street. But Italian-style gelato has captured this city's heart. On a warm summer evening, it's not unusual to see a long lineup outside **Mondo Gelato** (1094 Denman Street, West End, 604-647-6638; and 1222 Robson Street, Downtown, 604-694-0108), or **Mum's** (849 Denman Street, West End, 604-681-1500).

Mondo is relatively new, and delivers fifty or sixty flavors of a variety of frozen desserts, including sorbet, soy, and yogurt. Mum's has been on Denman for almost two decades, producing its own sorbeto, gelato, and frozen yogurt. (It's also known for its Italian coffee, served in big bowl-cups.)

And then there's **Mario's Gelati** (www.mariosgelati.com). Mario Lo-Scerbo's story began at his grandfather's ice cream parlor in the town of Amato in southern Italy. Mario emigrated in 1962 and built a small factory in East Vancouver. In 1998, he opened a modern glass-façade factory on industrial East 1st Avenue, just south of Science World, replete with a ballroom on the top floor (ideal for Italian weddings).

I won't (or can't) tell you how many pints of Mario's hazelnut or tiramisu ice cream I've downed over the years. But I will say it's smooth and luscious, as are my favorite sorbets — raspberry, blackberry, and lemon. Mario's produces dozens of flavors, including oddballs like Stilton and green tea. You can consume or take away these and other desserts, including soy-based Tofulati, at the street-level café, **Amato Gelato** (88 East 1st Avenue, Central Vancouver, 604-879-9011).

For those who insist on staggering variety, make your way to the oddly located **La Casa Gelato** (1033 Venables Street, East Vancouver, 604-251-3211, www.lacasagelato.com). La Casa boasts almost 200 ice cream, gelati ("je-lah-tee"), sorbetti, and yogurt "sensations." "Everything we got here," says indomitable owner Vince Maceo.

Suitably close to the beach sits **Paradiso Italian Gelato** (1520 Yew Street, Kitsilano, 604-738-4788). Everything here is made on the site from scratch, including a crème caramel, and orange, carrot, and lemon sorbetti.

S E C R E T

GOLF
✤

Even to a non-golfer like me, it's no news that **Fraserview Golf Course** (7800 Vivian Drive, South Vancouver, 604-280-1818, all city courses at www.vancouver.ca/parks) is the best of the city's three excellent 18-hole public courses. By the agreement of golf magazines, it's also one of the best courses in the country. On a fine summer day, this course in the city's semi-pastoral southeast quadrant is golf heaven. Walkers can enjoy it too; a well-tended path encircles the entire tree-framed site.

McCleery Golf Course is flush with the North Arm of the Fraser River (7188 Macdonald Street, Westside, 604-280-1818); **Langara**

Golf Course is smack in the city's south center (6706 Albert Street, off 49th Avenue, South Vancouver, 604-280-1818).

Vancouver's mild climate allows for year-round golfing, and while not everyone likes to putt in a drizzle, many apparently don't mind one bit. When it pours, you can always retreat to a clubhouse and restaurant. The Vancouver Board of Parks and Recreation has spent many millions fixing drainage and updating the facilities on all three courses.

The board also operates pitch-and-putt courses at **Queen Elizabeth Park** (Central Vancouver, 604-874-8336) and **Rupert Park** (3401 East 1st Avenue, East Vancouver, 604-257-8364) — the latter with great views of the mountains. But the best, says parks board spokeswoman Terri Clark, is the one near the south entrance to **Stanley Park** (2099 Beach Avenue, 604-681-8847), in the Ted and Mary Grieg Rhododendron Garden. Of this location in spring, Clark says: "The colors and wafting scents in and around each fairway make this one of the most beautiful pitch-and-putts in the world. I kid you not."

If you have wheels, the **Burnaby Mountain Golf Course** is a scenic and reasonably priced option (7600 Halifax Avenue, Burnaby, 604-280-7355, www.golfburnaby.net).

Northlands Golf Course in North Vancouver is gorgeously sited at the foot of the mountains and challenging; it was named best new Canadian course a few years back. From the Upper Levels Highway, take exit 22 to the Mount Seymour Parkway and follow the signs. For tee times, call 604-280-1111; www.golfnorthlands.com.

Finally, **Gleneagles Golf Course** is a public nine-hole gem tucked between the mountains and the ocean near Horseshoe Bay (6190 Marine Drive, West Vancouver, 604-921-7353, www.gleneaglesgolf.com). It's not long (par thirty-five) and it has its trials — the third

hole is aptly named Cardiac Hill. However, it's lush, pretty, and, I'm told, fun to play. It's also relatively cheap (as are the city's public courses).

S E C R E T

GRAFFITI

Graffiti is scribbled throughout the city, although civic and private crews do a fairly good job of keeping it under control. However, all hell is allowed — or even encouraged — to break loose in a small pocket of a semi-abandoned industrial zone just east of Main Street, around **Station Street** and **Prior Street** (East Vancouver).

Here, on almost every surface — cement, wood, corrugated iron, and Dumpster — taggers and graffiti artists have gone to work. The cumulative effect is, for better or worse, a kind of outdoor graffiti gallery.

A few buildings have been spared. The 1919 neo-Classical Pacific Central Station (1150 Station Street), where Via Rail, Amtrak, and long-distance bus services operate, has been either zealously guarded or instantly repainted. The historic Ivanhoe Hotel, always a rough spot in the heart of graffiti-ville, has been transformed into a low-budget backpacker's haven, the **Central Station Hostel** (1038 Main Street, 604-681-9118), and at last visit had a gorgeous new coat of paint, with not a tag to be seen.

However, every other building or wall within a two- or three-block radius, and particularly eastward into the railway warehouse district, is plastered with this deliberately cryptic form of expression.

Interestingly, the Cobalt Hotel (917 Main Street), which in the past competed with the Ivanhoe for notoriety, recently installed a large sign drawn in the universal script of graffiti aficionados that reads "Vancouver's Hardcore Bar." Among the victims of graffiti-ville is a small neo-Classical bank building, long abandoned at the corner of Main Street and Prior Street.

If you doubt anyone ever sees this stuff, take a look at the hoardings on Prior Street, dutifully plastered with multiple posters for indie music events. Or hang about on Station Street at dusk, or in mid-afternoon, and witness the quiet deals taking place.

Another feature of the area is a memorial to the fourteen female engineering students shot on December 6, 1989, at the University of Montreal. Titled *Marker of Change*, the large circle of fourteen stone benches is graffiti-free. It's set among the trees of Thornton Park, directly across from Pacific Central Station, and was the subject of enormous controversy during the planning process.

SECRET

GRANVILLE ISLAND

Granville Island (www.granvilleisland.com) is no secret. But it's easy to get stuck in and around the public market or the square outside the delectable pastry-making **La Baguette et L'Echalote** (1680 John-ston Street, 604-684-1351, www.labaguettebakery.com) and overlook the island's hidden charms and byways.

I suggest starting at the extreme eastern end, at a manmade grassy knoll known as **The Mound**, which has a rough-hewn amphi-

theater where buskers and others perform in summer. Walk counter-clockwise along the wooden seaside boardwalk, past the Granville Island Hotel, and you'll come to a towering, bright yellow, seven-ton crane with a wooden hut atop. It's one of the few reminders of a time, from the 1920s to the 1960s, when this island was a clanking, smoking center of sawmills, ironworks, and other industrial activity. A working railway once bisected the island; you can still see the tracks as you walk around.

Today, the work goes on in the form of artisans and craftspeople, many of whom have studios in the central part of the island. They include **Joel Berman Glass Studios** (1244 Cartwright Street, 604-684-8332, www.jbermanglass.com).

Marine life is an important island theme, and the **Maritime Market** runs along the southwest shoreline. But back on Cartwright at the **Alder Bay Boat Company** (1247 Cartwright Street, 604-685-1730), you can see craftsmen making perfect classical rowboats, as well as small sailboats and canoes. The company figures prominently in the annual Vancouver International Wooden Boat Festival, held on the island in late August.

From here, cut west through Railspur Park to Railspur Alley, the most recent addition to Granville Island and artisan heaven. Tenants include a luthier, a gifted folk artist with heaps of attitude (**Peter Kiss Gallery**, 1327 Railspur Alley, 604-696-0433, www.peterkiss.com); woodworkers, a leather maker, and a silversmith; and several shops, including **Alarté** (1369 Railspur Alley, 604-879-7235), selling hand-painted scarves in the many colors of an ancient rainbow. There's also **i.e. creative** (1399 Railspur Alley, 604-254-4374, www.iecreative.com), which produces oddball items that are, well, hugely creative.

Island nooks and crannies deliver treasures: west of Ocean Cement,

follow the boardwalk and you'll come to **The Silk Weaving Studio**
(1531 Johnston Street, 604-687-7455, www.silkweavingstudio.com),
with weavers at work on their looms, and garments for sale or to order. And around the island's west side are shops and galleries selling
the output of some of BC's best artists. They include the **Dundarave
Print Workshop and Gallery** (1640 Johnston Street, 604-689-
1650, www.dundaraveprintworkshop.ca); **Malaspina Printmak-
ers Studio and Gallery** (1555 Duranleau Street, 604-688-1827);
Gallery of BC Ceramics (1359 Cartwright Street, 604-669-3606,
www.bcpotters.com); **Crafthouse** (1386 Cartwright Street, 604-
687-7270; www.cabc.net); and the **Federation of Canadian Artists**
gallery (1241 Cartwright Street, 604-681-8534). These premises support both veteran and up-and-coming artists, and you won't look far
before stumbling on masterpieces.

S E C R E T

GREEK
✤

The city's Greek community, while modest in size, has a strong
presence. Maybe that's because it got off to a heady start when
members of the Pantages family, builders of those fabulous Art Deco
vaudeville houses around North America early in the 20th century,
made the city their home. By the 1920s and '30s, Greek cafés and
markets flourished; by the '50s, Greeks had made Kitsilano, particularly the Broadway corridor, their territory. Restaurants, meeting
places such as billiard halls, and food stores remain.

Although it suffered several fires, **Parthenon Importers** (3080 West

Broadway, Kitsilano, 604-733-4191) rose phoenix-like and remains a popular market for all foods Greek. Here, you'll find twenty varieties of olives (including feta-stuffed), nut-rich baklava and Easter-style panettone, inexpensive tins of oil-soaked dolmades, and pastas and cheeses.

Broadway and 4th Avenue offer a good selection of Greek eateries. **Simpatico Ristorante** (2222 West 4th Avenue, Kitsilano, 604-733-6824) has been here so long people go back out of sheer habit. More to my liking is "Zagat-rated" **Ouzeri** (3189 West Broadway, Kitsilano, 604-739-9378, www.ouzeri.ca), at a bright corner location. Also popular is the casual **Kalamata Greek Taverna** (388 West Broadway, Central Vancouver, 604-872-7050).

But Greek restaurants can, in my view, be overpriced. Fans of the cuisine like me have been looking eastward for less expensive fare. I suggest **The Main** (4210 Main Street, East Vancouver, 604-709-8555, www.mainonmain.com). This largish restaurant serves up a hip yet authentic atmosphere, classic dishes, and prices that put some west-side eateries to shame. A similar place for relatively cheap Greek fare is **Tsolias Taverna** (2217 East Hastings Street, East Vancouver, 604-251-6010).

Greek restaurants in the West End are also known, in part, for their modest prices and popularity — particularly **Takis Taverna** (1106 Davie Street, 604-682-1336) and **Stepho's Greek Taverna** (1124 Davie Street, 604-683-2555).

Suburban Ladner is the perfect little village for an evening stroll, and the Greek eatery comes highly recommended: **Taverna Gorgona** (4857 Elliott Street, Ladner, 604-946-9111, www.tavernagorgona.com).

While there are several Greek churches around town, including a small historic cathedral just off Main Street, the largest gathering place is **St. George's Greek Orthodox Cathedral** and the **Hellenic Community Centre** (4500 Arbutus Street, Westside, 604-266-7148). A few years back, when the Patriarch of the Greek Orthodox Church visited Vancouver, the Greek community asked city council to break with policy and rename adjacent Valley Drive after him. Some city councilors balked at the idea. A compromise was struck. Look for the yellow street sign on what remains Valley Drive: "Patriarch Bartholomew Way."

S E C R E T

GROUSE GRIND

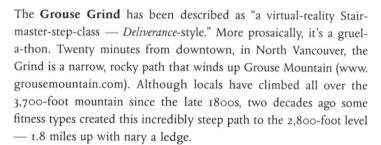

The **Grouse Grind** has been described as "a virtual-reality Stairmaster-step-class — *Deliverance*-style." More prosaically, it's a gruel-a-thon. Twenty minutes from downtown, in North Vancouver, the Grind is a narrow, rocky path that winds up Grouse Mountain (www.grousemountain.com). Although locals have climbed all over the 3,700-foot mountain since the late 1800s, two decades ago some fitness types created this incredibly steep path to the 2,800-foot level — 1.8 miles up with nary a ledge.

Since then, the Grind has become an ultimate test of physical and psychological endurance. "Don't even think about it if you're not in reasonable shape," veterans warn. But every year, as many as 100,000 people do, although not all succeed — and few do so at record speeds of well under one hour. The reward? Pride, relief, a stiff drink at the patio bar at the top (if you're legal drinking age — I've heard of four-year-old climbers), and a gondola trip back down.

The trail deteriorates in winter and is costly to maintain. At press time, its ownership remained, well, up in the air. The business that operates most Grouse Mountain facilities and concessions would like to buy or manage it. However, for the time being, the Greater Vancouver Regional District owns and maintains it at public expense.

In 1999, a hiker died in an avalanche-related accident on the trail. Since then, it has been closed in winter. Unfortunately, the fence and gate don't prevent would-be grinders from making their way around and onto the trail before the snow is completely melted.

Out-of-bounds mountain activity — particularly snowboarding and impromptu hiking by the ill-prepared — results in a number of deaths every year. It also creates incredible work for volunteers of the North Shore Rescue Society, who endlessly search the woods and gullies by foot and helicopter, often in the early hours of very cold mornings, for lost souls.

SECRET

HAIRCUTS

Vancouver claims the dubious distinction of landing "Canada's first blow-dry bar." So if you want your hair blow-dried — in any style, from punk to classy straight — in less than 30 minutes, make your way to **Blo Yaletown** (1150 Hamilton Street, Yaletown, 604-909-9495, www.blomedry.com). Blo also has salons — no, more like lounges — in South Granville and at the Four Seasons Hotel downtown.

The cheapest cuts in the city are to be had at **Vancouver Com-**

munity College's City Centre campus (250 West Pender Street, Downtown, 604-443-8332). It's well under ten bucks for a shampoo, cut, and blow-dry. Or check out the row of cheap salons in the 600 block of Main Street in Chinatown. They're busy, but employees are still out on the street, eyeing your cut and enticing you in.

At the other extreme, the hyper-hip and those with sizable disposable incomes get their hair, nails, faces, and bodies well worked over at **Tech 1 Hair Design Inc.** (1057 Cambie Street, Yaletown, 604-689-1202, www.tech1hairdesign.com).

S E C R E T

HEMP

At a busy industrial intersection not far off Commercial Drive you'll find **HT Naturals**, formerly Hemptown Clothing (1307 Venables Street, East Vancouver, 604-255-5055, www.htnaturals.com). Originally a seller of hemp T-shirts and golf shirts, the firm now markets organic and "eco" textiles made from bamboo, soy, cotton and, still, hemp. The apparel division, NAT, produces an expanding range of casual, even fashionable, clothing for men and women.

SECRET

HERBALISTS

Herbal medicine is found in health shops and mainstream food markets such as Capers and Choices around the city. But traditional Chinese herbalists continue to hold their own in Chinatown and elsewhere in the Lower Mainland, and people of every background seek them out.

One of the oldest in the city is the **Beijing Trading Co.** (89 East Pender Street, Chinatown, 604-684-3563). Typical of traditional herbalists, the business has a long wall stocked, top to bottom, with large containers of medicinal ingredients — everything from seahorse to ginseng in dozens of forms. Orders are mixed at the counter by trained practitioners. At a desk behind the counter sits Dr. Hong Wei-Xian, a Guangzhou-trained doctor with all the documents to prove it (he's also an acupuncturist). Dr. Hong will diagnose your ailment, write a prescription, see it filled in the shop, give you careful instructions on taking it, and expect you to return to see him if it doesn't do the job intended.

HIKING AND WALKING

Given the seemingly unending landscape of mountains, peaks, glaciers, lakes, and valleys that runs north along the coast, coupled with a gorgeous river and ocean shoreline around and south of the city, it's no surprise that hiking (or just "walking," as the English call it) is hugely popular.

Mountain Equipment Co-op (130 West Broadway, Central Vancouver, 604-872-7858; also 1341 Main Street, North Vancouver, 604-990-4417, www.mec.ca) does a staggering business in footwear, rainwear, fleeces, packs, trekking poles, compasses, and compact binoculars — for starters. Actually, this mega-market is as much a resource center as a business. You'll find books on hiking and climbing, and lots of staffers in the know.

An ideal place to begin hiking is **Cypress Provincial Park** and adjoining **Hollyburn Mountain** in West Vancouver (see "Secret Hollyburn Mountain"), or **Mount Seymour Provincial Park**, reachable from the Mount Seymour Parkway in North Vancouver.

BC **Parks** has published an excellent map titled *Provincial Parks of the Lower Mainland.* It includes these and other superb (though a little more distant) parks, such as **Golden Ears Park** east of the city, and **Alice Lake** and **Garibaldi** provincial parks north of Squamish.

For provincial park information, go to www.gov.bc.ca and the pages headed BC Parks, or call 604-924-2200 (in the Lower Mainland) or 604-898-3678 (Garibaldi-Sunshine Coast).

An easy way to get to know the region's hiking potential while safely testing your abilities is to join the **North Shore Hikers** (www. northshorehikers.org). A well-organized group with a long history in southwest BC, it runs hikes of varying degrees of difficulty (or ease) almost every Saturday and Sunday of the year. Locations are as diverse and distant as the Joffre Lakes north of Whistler and the Mount Baker region in Washington state. However, most of its hikes are relatively close to Vancouver, and several are to inner-city locations such as Stanley Park. A modest yearly membership fee is involved.

If you want to take the North Shore mountains at one fell swoop, consider the **Baden-Powell Trail**, wending twenty-five miles from Deep Cove in Indian Arm to Horseshoe Bay on Howe Sound, and reaching to almost 4,000 feet on Black Mountain. This spectacular trail, opened in 1971, takes in (from east to west) the steep terrain of Indian Arm and Seymour Mountain; Lynn Canyon and Valley; Grouse Mountain; Mosquito Creek (relax, it's just a name); the Capilano River, canyon, and lake; Cypress Bowl; and Hollyburn and Black mountains — the entire terrain. Do the trail end to end, and you'll never regret it. Among several good hiking books is *109 Walks in British Columbia's Lower Mainland*, published by Greystone Books. However, it covers only the frequently traveled eastern portion of the Baden-Powell Trail.

North Vancouver's **Lynn Canyon Park** includes a suspension bridge over a 166-foot canyon that rivals the touristy Capilano Suspension Bridge — but without the crowds and entry fee. The park is off the Upper Levels Highway and Lynn Valley Road; follow the signs to the Lynn Canyon Ecology Centre. Beyond the bridge are dozens of trails through the canyon park and into **Lynn Headwaters Regional Park**.

For the less physically adventurous, there's lots of easy hiking and walking within the metropolitan region that you can reach in a short drive or even by public transit (see "Secret Walks with Charles Clapham").

Metro Vancouver, covering Greater Vancouver, oversees twenty parks with a total area of 28,000 acres, all within an hour's drive of central Vancouver. They include gems such as **Capilano River** in North Vancouver, **Boundary Bay** in Delta, **Minnekhada** in Pitt Meadows, and **Pacific Spirit Park** on the end of the Point Grey peninsula. You can download detailed maps at www.metrovancouver. org, but it's easier to invest in a good city map and just find your way there.

If it's wet or blustery, the weather can be drier south of the Fraser River. Spectacular, if relatively easy, hikes and walks include the 12 miles of ocean and river dikes (suitable for cycling, too) around the perimeter of west and south **Richmond**, and the Iona sewage outfall in **Iona Beach Regional Park**. The latter may sound uninviting, but this straight-ahead walk of almost three miles plunks you smack in the middle of ocean and river, seemingly at the foot of the coastal mountains. After crossing the Arthur Laing Bridge from Vancouver, you'll see a directional sign on the roundabout. Travel northward again, then westward along the island spit.

Richmond's dikes are accessible at road ends around the municipality, but particularly at the south end of No. 2 Road and on River Road. For details on these and other nature trails in Richmond, go to www. richmond.ca.

SECRET

HOLLYBURN
MOUNTAIN

While a series of mountains spans the North Shore, from the Lions peaks in the northwest to Mount Seymour in the east, **Hollyburn Mountain** (West Vancouver) remains the most historic, overlooked, and enticing summit for those in search of an out-of-the-way yet close-to-the-city experience.

Rising above the western portion of West Vancouver to 4,345 feet, Hollyburn Ridge and Mountain were recently incorporated into **Cypress Provincial Park**, which is accessible via Cypress Bowl Road from exit 8 on the Upper Levels Highway. This zigzagging road, offering spectacular views of the city, ends at the Cypress Bowl downhill ski center. You can reach the Hollyburn area by taking the turnoff before the end of the road — watch for the signs for cross-country skiing.

Hollyburn has been a popular ski destination since early in the last century. It remains centered on historic **Hollyburn Lodge**, which was built in the 1920s and, amazingly enough, is still serving burgers and hot chocolate to cross-country skiers and snowshoers. It closes at the end of the winter season, so hikers must pack in their lunches, but the lodge is worth a visit — it's literally held together with baling wire.

The entire Hollyburn area retains a 1930s through 1950s ambiance, which includes dozens of simple wood-frame cabins with split-shingle roofs and stove-pipe chimneys that mock the luxury and accessibility of their Whistler counterparts.

The habitat takes in undulating meadows, a series of tiny lakes (First, West, Fourth, and so on), and a network of trails that wends through stands of aged hemlock and yellow cedar.

Hikers and snowshoers can ascend a series of trails to Hollyburn peak (allow three hours for the return trip), where you'll experience unimpeded views of the Garibaldi and Lions mountains to the northwest, the city and Cascade range to the south, and Georgia Strait to the Gulf Islands and Vancouver Island.

The lack of modern amenities on Hollyburn (they're found in the Cypress Bowl ski area, and on Grouse and Seymour mountains) is part of its charm. Here pesky Whisky Jacks will compete for the opportunity to eat from your hand — one aspect of a mountain culture that has existed here for more than a century. (Hollyburn was named by West Van settler John Lawson in the early 1900s, after he planted holly trees by the "burn," or stream, that ran down through his property.)

Cypress Bowl Recreation Ltd., which leases part of the park from the government, posts maps of cross-country and snowshoeing routes at www.cypressmountain.com. No mention is made of hiking, because hikers don't generate revenue. However, the maps can be interpreted for summer use.

Another source of information is the BC government Web site (www.gov.bc.ca, see pages headed BC **Parks**). Here, you'll find detailed trail descriptions and a downloadable map that includes what were once logging access roads and virtually every trail, lake, and peak.

Sigge's Sport Villa (2077 West 4th Avenue, Kitsilano, 604-731-8818, www.sigges.com) sells and rents cross-country and snowshoe equipment.

SECRET
HOME STUFF

Expensive furnishing outlets abound, but here are a few places with unusual offerings at modest prices.

Blue Terra Designs (1146 Commercial Drive, East Vancouver, 604-253-1711) sells Indonesian and Moroccan furnishings and accessories. Stock includes artsy mood lamps, sconce lanterns, bamboo whatevers, tree-skin mats, and furniture of recycled teak.

Dream Designs (956 Commercial Drive, East Vancouver, 604-254-5012, www.dreamdesigns.ca) offers collectibles such as North African basket-bowls, Indian canisters, and decorative Burmese pots. But Dream is more widely known for its natural futons and covers, and white and bleached cottons, twills, flannels, and silks sold by the yard (or meter). It also sells yoga and meditation cushions, and soy, hemp, and beeswax candles.

Bravura Interiors (534 West Pender Street, Downtown, 604-872-4880, www.greatpacificfurniture.com) handles ultra-modern Italian imports — a kind of upscale IKEA at east-side prices. Particularly fetching are cushiony, hand-stitched leather couches from a European firm called Calia.

SECRET

INDULGENCES

At **Morton's Steak House** (750 West Cordova Street, Downtown, 604-915-5105, www.mortons.com), the consumption of huge, gorgeous cuts of beef or oversized shrimps is a way of life. Of course, you have to be able to afford it, and the prices can make your eyes bulge (or ears swell — serving staff do an astounding menu presentation). But cut into that Double Cut filet mignon or New York steak and you'll understand what it's about: everything about this place is hedonistic, from the service through the desserts. I mean, Double Chocolate Mousse?

For a pre-dinner aperitif in a plush room where everyone but you (no, I should speak for myself) will appear to be famous, rich, or just ultra-fashionable, make for the **Bacchus Restaurant and Lounge** in the **Wedgewood Hotel** (845 Hornby Street, Downtown, 604-608-5319, www.wedgewoodhotel.com). A glass of wine costs as much as I pay for a bottle, but what the heck.

Lumiere (2551 West Broadway, Kitsilano, 604-739-8185, www.lumiere.ca) keeps topping the "best" lists — for all-round restaurant, high-end, French, and so on. Chef Dale MacKay, who came to Vancouver from Gordon Ramsay's celebrated London restaurant at the NYC Hotel, has replaced founding chef Rob Feenie, and this elegant room has acquired Relais & Chateaux Gourmand status. Expect exceptional dining and wining—and be ready to pay for it.

Chasing Lumiere in the upscale-eateries popularity stakes is **West** (2881 Granville Street, Central Vancouver, 604-738-8938, www.westrestaurant.com). Named one of the "ten best restaurants worldwide" by the UK's *Independent* newspaper, it remains at the pinnacle of dining here. Chef Warren Geraghty (London and Michelin background) will deliver the likes of seared Qualicum Bay scallops with buttered lentils and pineau des charents, and the desserts — well, the desserts. Let's keep it simple. What about panettone with crème caramel?

Looking for a made-to-measure Italian-leather jacket — neatly fitted or bomber-style — in a forest green or soft maroon? **Ocean Drive** (1026 Mainland Street, Yaletown, 604-647-2244, www.oceandriveleather. com), favored by the film crowd, makes its garments on the premises and ships anywhere in the world that you and your credit card desire.

For accommodation, don't think you can do much better than a northwestward-looking room at the **Pan Pacific Hotel** (999 Canada Place, Downtown, 604-662-8111, www.panpacific.com).

I'll cap this with the ultimate indulgence — an evening of sweets from the Chocolate Bar at the Sutton Place Hotel's **Fleuri Restaurant** (845 Burrard Street, Downtown, 604-642-2900; call ahead for times and booking). Embracing everything from crêpes to frozen desserts and fancy cakes, the event can be enjoyed after dinner, or as a momentous meal in itself. The price is $26.

SECRET

INLINE SKATING

I was surprised to learn that Florida-based *Fitness and Speed Skating Times* recently named Vancouver the third-best North American destination for inline skating. The only reasoning I can come up with is the seawall (see "Secret Seawall") around much of the downtown peninsula — even though inline skaters occasionally clash with other users of the route — and some "skate-friendly" routes in the central city. However, the fact that skaters like the steep, curving roads on Seymour and Cypress mountains may have something to do with it.

Legally, in the City of Vancouver, inline skaters must use the roads rather than sidewalks, where there's no designated skating route. How this pans out only those brave enough to contend with traffic can say, but I've seen these guys travel down Burrard Street as fast as vehicles, so it must be working for some of them.

Tourists and English-language students — particularly, it seems, the Japanese — routinely rent inline skates. You can get them at **Spokes Stanley Park Bicycle Rentals** (1798 West Georgia Street, West End, 604-688-5141, www.vancouverbikerental.com). Spokes also supplies bikes for every age and ability — from one-speed cruisers to hybrid city bikes and tandems, and runs bike tours to Stanley Park and False Creek. **Bayshore Bicycles and Rollerblade Rentals** (745 Denman Street, West End, 604-688-2453, www.bayshorebikerentals.ca) rents inline skates, along with mountain, kids', and tandem bikes. You can even rent tennis racquets, and jogging and baby strollers. **Bikes 'N Blades Rental** (718 Denman Street, West End, 604-602-9899) also equips bikes with seats and trailers for the very young.

Those who take to these activities might do well to buy secondhand inline skates at **Cheapskates-Nineteen** (3496 Dunbar Street, West-side, 604-734-1160) or a bike at **Cheapskates Too** (3228 Dunbar Street, Westside, 604-734-1191). These consignment stores will take the items back when you're ready to move on to fancier equipment.

Reckless (1810 Fir Street, Central Vancouver, 604-731-2420) rents bikes of all sizes, car racks, backpacks, and panniers; a second location (110 Davie Street, Yaletown, 604-648-2600, www.rektek. com) supplies bikes and skates.

SECRET

INTERNET

Internet access is everywhere these days, so I won't provide a lot of listings. You can even access it free at the downtown **Vancouver Public Library** (350 West Georgia Street, Downtown, 604-331-3600) and most branch libraries, although you may have to wait for a terminal.

On high-traffic Davie Street in the accessible West End, there's **DowntownComputer** (1072 Davie Street, 604-682-5272) and its parent outlet, the **Downtown Computer Centre** (1035 Davie Street, 604-682-5240), for computer repairs and upgrades. This neighborhood is also home to **Internet Coffee** (1104 Davie Street, 604-682-6668, open to the early morning).

Blenz Coffee (www.blenz.com) currently has 27 outlets — all with wireless Internet — in the city, and more in the suburbs (among them: 338 Helmcken Street, Yaletown, 604-609-2768 and 700 Davie Street, West End, 604-633-1054, both with patio seating).

SECRET

IRISH

For reasons that remain unfathomable to me, Irish places are enormously popular in this city. The weekend lineup of under-thirty folks outside **Blarney Stone** (216 Carrall Street, Gastown, 604-687-4322, www.blarneystone.ca) routinely snakes along this somewhat seedy stretch of sidewalk.

The Irish Heather is more than a Gastown institution, it's a certifiable Presence. Recently the historic gastro pub moved across Carrall Street, and took with it its **Shebeen Whiskey House** (re-ensconced in an atmospheric space behind the bar-restaurant), as well as a deli/charcuterie called the **Salty Tongue** (Irish Heather and Shebeen, 212 Carrall Street; Salty Tongue, 210 Carrall Street, Gastown, 604-688-9779, www.irishheather.com). The Irish Heather is also behind the hugely successful **Salt** tasting room (see Secret Charcuteries).

There's also a nice old-wood atmosphere at **Morrissey Irish Bar and Restaurant** (1227 Granville Street, Downtown, 604-682-0909) and 10 beers, including Guinness and Kilkenny, on tap. This is something of a hangout for after-work types, music buffs, and, apparently, groups of women who like to be left alone. It also serves food of an un-Irish variety, such as wings and ribs.

SECRET

ITALIAN

❀

Nowhere will you find more genuine Italiana than at **Tosi Italian Food Imports** (624 Main Street, Chinatown, 604-681-5740). Given the area's volatility (to put it nicely) you must ring a buzzer to be let in. But in a moment or two, you'll enter a large, dimly lit grocery that hasn't changed one iota since Angelo Tosi's father opened it here in 1906. And while you may not care to stock up on one of fifty Pagani pastas, montasio cheese, various barrel-marinated olives, or the best oils and vinegars this side of Tuscany, you'll relish the atmosphere right out of *The Postman* — and genial wool-capped Angelo, who'll cut you a rich, glistening slab of farm-fresh parmesan to your specifications.

Italian provisioners are dotted throughout Vancouver. Several are found in the mixed Asian and European neighborhoods around Nanaimo Street and Hastings Street.

Renzullo Food Market (1370 Nanaimo Street, East Vancouver, 604-255-9655) is known for its antipasti and olives. **Ugo and Joe's** (2404 East Hastings Street, East Vancouver, 604-253-6844) specializes in cheeses and imported meats. The **Italian Meat Market and Deli** (2276 East Hastings Street, East Vancouver, 604-255-2032) is a picture-perfect deli with sausages, pastas, and cheeses to die for, as well as a meat-stuffed capon-roll that a neighbor claims is "world famous." Across the street, **Bianca-Maria Italian Foods** (2469 East Hastings Street, 604-253-9626) is run by knowing women with one foot in the old country.

On the Drive, **La Grotta del Formaggio** (1791 Commercial Drive,

East Vancouver, 604-255-3911) is a favorite of many. Like most of the above, it sells everything from artichokes to espresso makers, along with fine Italian oils, vinegars, pastas, sausages, and, of course, cheeses.

Both coffeehouse and delicatessen, **Epicurean** (1898 West 1st Avenue, Kitsilano, 604-731-5370) has built an enviable reputation for both its food and European ambiance. It's now licenced.

A short-lived secret, **The Italian Kitchen** (1037 Alberni Street, Downtown, 604-687-2858, www.theitaliankitchen.com) is an up-scale, happening option for anyone interested in a modern, interpretation of Italian. The bar and open-concept kitchen is a great place for singles and casual interlopers; the upstairs is slightly more formal (but still nicely laid back; its huge windows relate to the lively upper stories along Alberni Street. A pasta platter (sharing is encouraged) might feature spaghetti and meatballs with agnollotti stuffed with squash and mascarpone pappardelle, lamb sausage and more. The carpaccio pizza loads on the shaved beef tenderloin, asiago, pesto and baby argula. You get the picture. A toned down and more casual version of the same restaurant (both from the Glowbal Group) is the **Trattoria Italian Kitchen** (1850 West 4th Avenue, Kitsilano, www.trattoriakitchen.ca).

If you're the type who shuns quiet, decorous restaurants in favor of clattering plates, paper bibs, tightly packed tables, and all-round hustle, you'll love **Nick's Spaghetti House** (631 Commercial Drive, East Vancouver, 604-254-5633). Owned for more than fifty years by Nick and Paulina Felicella, this kitschy room packs 'em in night after night with huge platters of spaghetti and meatballs, linguini, cannelloni, and so on. House wines come by the "double glass" and half liter. Desserts run to a hefty cheesecake and sinful slab of tiramisu doused with chocolate. Another reliable haunt on The Drive, with wood-burning oven, is **Lombardo's Ristorante and Pizzeria** (1641 Commercial Drive, East Vanvouver, 604-251-2240). Also try longtime **Cipriano's Ristorante and Pizzeria** (3995 Main Street, Mount Pleasant, East Vancouver, 604-879-0020).

SECRET
JAPANESE
CONFECTIONS

For Japanese junk food, and a brief immersion into the world of the itinerant Japanese English-language student, visit **Minna No Konbiniya** (1238 Robson Street, Downtown, 604-682-3634). Something of a general store, it carries phenomenally popular sweets on themes such as Pocky and Hello Kitty; comfort food such as packaged ramen, dried fish, and rice crackers; huge sacks of Japanese rice; and tiny pink and lime-green umbrellas and teddy bears. There's also an Internet station. Upstairs in the **Karaoke Box** (604-688-0611), you'll find walls of movie videos, pool tables, a games arcade — and private rooms in which you can hunker down with Japanese, Cantonese, Korean, or English-language music and wail your heart out.

SECRET

JAPANESE CULTURE
❋

Vancouver's strong connection with Japan dates to the late 1800s, when Japanese men came over to work in the lumber industry. And before World War II, during which thousands of Japanese-Canadians were forcibly relocated to other parts of BC and Canada, the community's base was **Powell Street**. It's still a peculiarly charming, if hopelessly rundown, thoroughfare in the Downtown Eastside, not far from the waterfront.

Today the area around Powell Street and Oppenheimer Park is beset with drug problems, and virtually all Japanese-Canadians live elsewhere in the city. But small signs of a Japanese presence remain — here and there a shop, restaurant, or Buddhist temple. There's also the **Japanese Hall** (475 Alexander Street, East Vancouver, 604-254-2551). This delightful white-plaster building, with its arched window frames and black-tile trim, was built in 1928 as a Japanese-language school. In recent years, the local Japanese community has built a somewhat overbearing addition with the same mandate.

Japanese tourists have long liked Vancouver, if mostly for its relative safety and cleanliness, and proximity to nature, skiing, and the Canadian Rockies. Many Japanese English-language students choose it over myriad other English-teaching destinations. They tend to live with families on the North Shore or in apartments in the West End. And while a pocket in the vicinity of Alberni Street and Burrard Street has been dubbed Little Tokyo for its tourist-related businesses, penny-pinching students tend to frequent restaurants and stores along westerly Robson Street and Denman Street.

SECRET

JAPANESE FOOD

Japanese cuisine, particularly sushi, can be found on almost every commercial street in the city. Near the high end of the (financial) food chain sits **En Cuisine** (4422 West 10th Avenue, Westside, 604-730-0330). Owner Yami Yamagishi is touted as a gifted chef who skillfully unites Japanese tradition with French and Italian. His presentation — perhaps a circle-like rack of lamb with sour-plum rice, or folded petals of smoked salmon — is amazing. As well as wines by the glass or bottle, En serves seven premium sakes.

For those on a budget, you can do worse than chase down **Sushi-boy** (409 West Broadway, Central Vancouver, 604-879-5236, www.sushiboyltd.com). The sushi here is familiar (California roll), cheap, and quickly prepared for take-out. And a ravenous backpacker or cyclist will feel right at home in this humble space, if they can squeeze through the door.

One Japanese eatery that tops several "favorite" lists, in part for its all-you-can-eat sushi, is **Tanpopo** (1122 Denman Street, West End, 604-681-7777). And speaking of popular, I mustn't omit high-end **Tojo's** (202–777 West Broadway, Central Vancouver, 604-872-8950). In the most-chic category, serving "new concept Japanese Cuisine," there's **Bistro Sakana** (1123 Mainland Street, Yaletown, 604-633-1280).

Eccentricity lives at **Opera Sushi** (1640 West Broadway, Central Vancouver, 604-737-1030), where chef Joseph E celebrates his love of the genre with the occasional aria, and a wall of LPS that reinforces the opera theme. A wide and otherwise conventional selection of sushi includes the Tosca roll of salmon and tuna.

Those into conveyor-belt sushi delivery might hop on the ultimate conveyor — the SkyTrain — to the Eaton Centre in Metrotown, and **Taisho** (4700 Kingsway, Burnaby, 604-435-1211). It's said to have the longest belt and best food among belt deliverers.

A Kitsilano-style outlet — all rustic wood and determinedly casual — is the **Octopus' Garden Sushi Bar** (1995 Cornwall Avenue, Kitsilano, 604-734-8971).

There are a number of Japanese eateries in the 700 block of Denman Street. You'll also find Japanese (basic sushi or trendy), Chinese, Korean, and Vietnamese restaurants in the 1600 and 1700 blocks of Robson Street, including several in the **Robson Public Market** (1610 Robson Street, West End, www.robsonpublicmarket.com). Homesick ESL students populate **Guu** (838 Thurlow Street, Downtown, 604-685-8817, www.guu-izakaya.com) for its low-priced Japanese comfort food (lots of stir-fries and hot pots).

Or load up your shopping cart with everything Japanese at **Fujiya Japanese Foods** (912 Clark Drive, East Vancouver, 604-251-3711) and cook at home. Here, you'll find seafood, seaweeds, a deli with sushi, bento boxes, strange bottled things, and rice goodies galore.

SECRET

JAZZ

The **Coastal Jazz and Blues Society** (box office at 316 West Sixth Avenue, Central Vancouver, 604-872-5200 or 1-888-438-5200, www.coastaljazz.ca.com) has organized, promoted, and stuck by a jazz scene that has waxed and waned, but now appears to be relatively strong. The society is best known for the Vancouver International Jazz Festival in late June and early July.

Tickets for CJBS-listed events — listed in its quarterly publication, *Looking Ahead* — are generally available through Ticketmaster (604-280-4444), and **Highlife Records** (1317 Commercial Drive, East Vancouver, 604-251-6964).

A current hot spot for jazz is **The Cellar Restaurant and Jazz Club** (3611 West Broadway, Kitsilano, 604-738-1959, www.cellarjazz. com), where jazz runs across the style spectrum. Credit local musician Cory Weeds, who helped to pull the city's jazz out of a blue funk by opening the space a few years back.

A slightly older crowd frequently packs **Rossini's** (1525 Yew Street, Kitsilano, 604-737-8080, www.rossinisjazz.com), which is otherwise something of a neighborhood bar-restaurant for musicians, writers, and related types.

Those who like their jazz progressive might head to the **Western Front** (303 East 8th Avenue, Mount Pleasant, East Vancouver, 604-876-9343, www.front.bc.ca). This rustic, rambling, and invitingly creaky all-wood building deserves a visit in its own right. Inside, you'll find the **Western Front Society**, long a guardian of the avant-garde and political arts; it's currently devoted to "the contemporary media arts and interdisciplinary practice." You get the picture. Attendance demands, well, open-mindedness — a recent performance involved a "giant grain elevator transformed into a musical instrument." But the Western Front also hosts more accessible jazz performed by emerging young artists from across Canada, Europe, and beyond.

S E C R E T

JEWISH
☙

The Vancouver Jewish community has a proud heritage in the Oppenheimer brothers, David and Isaac, who emigrated from Germany in the late 1800s. They founded a wholesale grocery business called Oppenheimer Brothers, today the city's oldest firm. At one time, they owned much of the downtown waterfront.

David proved both a tireless business promoter and a progressive four-term mayor of Vancouver. He established public services such as water supply, sewers, a fire department, street construction, schools, and parks, and helped found institutions such as the YMCA and Board of Trade. The Oppenheimers' presence is commemorated in **Oppenheimer Park** (between Powell Street and Cordova Street, East Vancouver). Though now a centerpiece of the city's poorest neighborhood, the area was once the hub of a new coastal metropolis.

A later wave of Jews from Eastern Europe settled in nearby Strathcona. The first synagogue, an odd Mediterranean-style structure at East Pender and Heatley streets, was built in the 1920s (it has since been converted to condos). By the 1960s, almost all the city's Jews had moved to the south-center of Vancouver. Oak Street has evolved into a Jewish thoroughfare, with large Orthodox, Conservative, and Reform temples still prominently marking the way. On Oak Street at West 41st Avenue, the community reaches its apotheosis with the **Jewish Community Centre** (950 West 41st Avenue, South Vancouver, 604-257-5111, www.jccgv.com), which includes a library, art gallery, public theater, and the Vancouver Holocaust Education Centre.

The area also has several good food stores. Start with **Kaplan's** deli and eatery (5775 Oak Street, South Vancouver, 604-263-2625, www.

kaplans.ca) for Montreal-style smoked meat, bar none. For basic kosher provisions, there's **Omnitsky Kosher** (5866 Cambie Street, South Vancouver, 604-321-1818) and **Sabra Kosher Restaurant and Bakery** (3844 Oak Street, Central Vancouver, 604-733-4912).

In recent decades, many young Jews have moved to the suburbs: an estimated twenty congregations, with small synagogues, thrive in communities such as Surrey, Coquitlam, and particularly Richmond. The *Western Jewish Bulletin*, now called **Jewish Independent** (www. jewishindependent.ca) one of Vancouver's oldest ethnic/religious community newspapers, remains a well-respected source of news.

S E C R E T

JUICE BARS

In 1999, a guy from Alberta, Dale Wishewan, started **Booster Juice** (www.boosterjuice.com), and today it has franchises across North America (while Wishewan has picked up numerous business awards). Which isn't to say it's been easy. Fruit juice bars have had their ups and downs and, at last report, there was but one Booster Juices (think fruit-rich power drinks) in Vancouver (UBC Marketplace, 2162 Western Parkway, University of British Columbia, 604-568-6603). Calgary-based **Jugo Juice** (www.jugojuice.com) has fared somewhat better, at least in Vancouver. With smoothies made from tree fruits (and perhaps a little wheatgrass blended in) the firm boasts 11 Vancouver outlets (including 1168 Davie Street, West End, 604-688-2444 and numerous downtown locations).

Being a fan of puréed fruits that aren't overly diluted with crushed ice, I'm always on the lookout for an uncompromising juice bar. The closest I've come is the **Fraser Valley Juice and Salad Bar** (Granville Island Public Market, 604-669-0727, www.fraservalleyjuice. com). This is nothing more than a market stall, but it's a good place to pick up a truly vegetarian lunch as well.

SECRET

KAYAKS AND CANOES

A half-hour drive from downtown Vancouver, you can slip into a two-person kayak for a paddle up Indian Arm. Genial Peter Loppe and his **Lotus Land Tours** (1-800-528-3531, www.lotuslandtours. com) organizes half-day kayaking trips, with picnic lunches (salmon, mulled wine). Best of all, from your kayak you get a duck's-eye view of the glorious setting where ocean meets rainforest. An easy paddle also takes in the old wooden buildings along this eleven-mile fjord — one of which has variously functioned as a brothel, remote hotel, and Prohibition-era liquor outlet.

Although most kayakers hang up their paddles in late autumn, some go out year round. If you're prepared to dress warmly, carry the essential safety equipment, paddle with a companion or two, and keep to the less windy waterways, you will experience life on the water at its most pristine in the off season. All of this does not come cheaply: outfitting a winter kayaker can cost hundreds of dollars. Then there's the kayak itself.

Ecomarine Ocean Kayak Centre (1668 Duranleau Street, Granville Island, 604-689-7575, www.ecomarine.com) runs what some say is the best ocean-kayaking school around. It rents single and double kayaks, as well as roof racks to carry your kayaks into the deep beyond.

Feathercraft Products (1244 Cartwright Street, Granville Island 604-681-8437, www.feathercraft.com) makes folding kayaks. These gorgeous, sinewy craft are modeled on 5,000-year-old hunting kayaks made of driftwood, whalebone, and sealskin. When you order a kayak, Feathercraft will shape it to fit your body. Then you can go out and kayak around the relatively quiet waters of False Creek, or collapse the kayak into a portable package (some fold down into backpacks), head across the Lions Gate Bridge, and steady yourself for a tumultuous plunge down the Capilano River.

Kayak and canoe enthusiasts might check out the **False Creek Community Centre** (1318 Cartwright Street, Granville Island, 604-257-8195, www.vancouver.ca/parks). This is a base for the **False Creek Racing Canoe Club** (www.fcrcc.com) and the focal point for seafaring paddle sports such as dragonboat racing, outrigger canoeing, and marathon and voyageur canoeing. It's also home to the perennial world-champion False Creek Women's Dragon Boat Team (note the arms on these well-toned women, who are often seen hanging about the center and dock, www.falsecreekwomen.com).

Another mecca for naturally powered watersports — dinghy and other small-boat sailing, windsurfing, paddling, rowing, and ocean kayaking — is the **Jericho Sailing Centre** (1300 Discovery Street, Westside, 604-224-4177). Operated by the Jericho Sailing Centre Association (www.jsca.bc.ca) at an enviable location on Locarno Beach, the center has its own fleet, which it rents out and uses for

teaching, regattas, and races. A number of clubs and teams also operate out of this former World War II aircraft hangar.

This is an all-age operation. Older people learn recreational sailing here, and life-jacketed toddlers experience their first rowboat. And on many a morning you'll catch sight of a team of muscular Hawaiian-style paddlers confronting the waves (and plunging into the water — it's part of their relay-style routine) in preparation for an international race in Hawaii.

SECRET

KIDS
❧

The Vancouver Board of Parks and Recreation (604-257-8400, www.vancouver.ca/parks) operates more than twenty community centers. These centers host a huge variety of other children's programs, courses, and individual and team sports for all ages, year round. They also hold a wide array of summer camps. Some of the more unusual ones — including kayaking, canoeing, and arts camps — are run out of the idiosyncratic **False Creek Community Centre** (1318 Cartwright Street, Granville Island, 604-257-8195, www.vancouver.ca/parks). Young children also revel in the **Waterpark**, adjacent to the community center. The idea is to get seriously soaked in the slides, geyser jets, sprays, and water cannons (or canyons). Nearby looms the **Kids Market**, an enticing emporium best avoided if either your wallet or your willpower is not in the best of shape.

Another water playground stands adjacent to the seawall on the north side of Stanley Park at **Lumberman's Arch**. And while the city has a number of pools suitable for children, the best by far is the **Maple Grove Pool** at Yew Street and Southwest Marine Drive (South Vancouver). Located in the leafy park of the same name, it features separate pools for children and toddlers.

The dubious distinction of being, for the moment, the only beanbag movie theater in Canada belongs to Famous Players' **SilverCity Coquitlam** (170 Schoolhouse Street, Coquitlam, off the Lougheed Highway, 604-523-2911). Instead of the standard movie house setting of rigid chairs, the front of one screening room features a cluster of beanbag chairs and sofas shaped like French fries, popcorn, hot dogs, hearts, and so on. There's also a gallery of distortion mirrors, and kids can move around during the showing. Only child-oriented films are shown.

Artistically inclined youngsters will find extraordinary resources at **Arts Umbrella** (1286 Cartwright Street, Granville Island, 604-681-5268, www.artsumbrella.com). Programs cover dance (classical ballet to hip-hop), theater (junior troupe to senior touring), visual arts (clay sculpture to digital filmmaking), and early childhood programs. Programs run year round, including summer.

Bard on the Beach, a phenomenally successfully producer of Shakespearean fare in Kitsilano's Vanier Park from June through September, runs workshops in July and August for young thespians (604-737-0625, www.bardonthebeach.org). The Young Shakespearean program includes movement, voice training, and Shakespearean language, all culminating in a public performance. Programs are tailored to ages eight to twelve, and thirteen to eighteen.

UBC's **Pacific Museum of the Earth** (Geological Services Centre, 6339 Stores Road, University of British Columbia, www.science. ubc.ca) is by no means designed for children, but they'll love the upright skeleton of an 80-million-year-old *Lambeosaurus* dinosaur in full running mode. **Maplewood Farm** (405 Seymour River Place,

North Vancouver, 604-929-5610, www.maplewoodfarm.bc.ca) is a five-acre haven for several hundred domestic animals and birds, and a favorite with the younger set. And while a day spent at that giant golf ball at the eastern end of False Creek known as **Science World** (1455 Quebec Street, Central Vancouver, 604-443-7443, www.scienceworld.ca) is my idea of being plunged into hell, children love it. Its **Omnimax Theatre** features exceptional films on nature themes. Another undying favorite (with kids and oldsters) is the **Stanley Park Miniature Railway** — see "Secret Trains" for more information.

Kidsbooks (3083 West Broadway, Kitsilano, 604-738-5335, www.kidsbooks.ca) sells so many titles that well-stocked categories include "Pioneer," "Slavery," "Exploration," and "The Wars." Dolls that you can be sure have been well vetted for political correctness — along with games, puppets (beaver and moose), puzzles, toys, CDs, videos, and more — fill these large premises.

Current city guidebooks for caregivers include *Kids' Vancouver*, from Raincoast Books, and *Jack Christie's Day Trips with Kids*, from Greystone Books.

SECRET

KITE-FLYING
✤

While fierce westerly winds can turn Georgia Street and other downtown corridors into freezing funnels or tunnels, these moody currents also provide for great sailing in Burrard Inlet and English Bay, and kite-flying in spacious **Vanier Park** on Kitsilano Point. A fine place to hang about in its own right, on a nice windy day this waterfront park attracts a bevy of flyers, from experts who handle multiple kites that perform like high-flying flocks of birds to beginners with lumbering quasi-windsocks.

Kites — from functional to decorative — can be had at **Kites on Clouds** (131 Water Street, Gastown, 604-669-5677) and **Kites and Puppets** in the Kids Market (1496 Cartwright Street, Granville Island, 604-685-9877, www.kitesandpuppets.ca). Here — among a wonderful jumble, much of it somehow suspended — longtime proprietor Sally Fontana includes workable kites shaped like a sailing ship or a hummingbird in flight.

SECRET

KITSILANO

To get a feeling for the quintessential Vancouver neighborhood, explore **Kitsilano**, lying along the south shore of outer Burrard Inlet, and otherwise bounded by Burrard Street, West 16th Avenue, and Alma Street. Originally inhabited by native Indians (and named for Chief Khahtsahlano), the area began metamorphosing in the late 1800s with the addition of sawmills and canneries. Through the twentieth century, it evolved from a shoreline cluster of family estates. Carpenter houses and Arts-and-Crafts bungalows spread south and eastward. Then the neighborhood became a low-rent hippie haven. Today, it's a mix of pretty costly yet (mostly) modest single-family houses and mid-range condominiums.

Walk along the shoreline from Vanier Park, through Kits Point and Kitsilano Park, then dip down to an odd extension of Point Grey Road (north of Cornwall) before resurfacing near Macdonald Street.

Along the way, you'll see the whole mix, from outwardly humble to seaside expensive. Then head south along Macdonald Street and past 4th Avenue as far as 7th Avenue for a remarkable row (on the west side of Macdonald) of typical West Coast workmen's houses, some of which still function as boarding houses. Then turn east again — along, say, 7th Avenue, but 6th or 5th are good, too. If you take your time, you'll experience the leafy, garden-y, post-hippie, community-minded Vancouver that many people value greatly. Alternatively, walk west from Macdonald Street along any avenue between Cornwall Avenue and 4th Avenue, and you'll enjoy much the same ambiance, though it's a little more upscale here.

SECRET
LATIN AMERICAN

Commercial Drive has long been the nexus for Spanish-speaking immigrants, mostly from Chile and Central America. It boasts a cluster of Latin American clubs and eateries, among them **Havana** (1212 Commercial Drive, East Vancouver, 604-253-9119, www. havanarestaurant.com). Its kitchen turns out tapas and entrées such as jambalaya, and snapper with mango salsa, preferably consumed on its all-weather patio. However, Havana also houses a backroom art gallery and sixty-seat theater (mainly alternative fare). Throw in a good bar and Cuban cigars, and you have a Caribbean-style night on the town.

The **Latin Quarter** (1305 Commercial Drive, East Vancouver, 604-251-1144), with a Peruvian owner and, at last report, Mexican chef, offers tapas (I like their crostini with goat cheese) and entrées. But just as important, a superior string-and-drum quartet plays wonderful edgy instrumental music nightly, followed by fine vocals. Sit for an hour or three, and you'll definitely mellow.

A delightful little Mexican restaurant that regularly appears on somebody's "best list" is **Tio Pepe's Restaurante** (1134 Commercial Drive, East Vancouver, 604-254-8999, www.tiopepes.com). The **Topanga Café** (2904 West 4th Avenue, Kitsilano, 604-733-3713) has also been dishing out Mexican dishes — specialties include carne nortena, tamales, huevos rancheros, and Mexican pizza — for a very long time, so it must be doing something right. A hugely successful Latin spot — a lounge with atmosphere and music — is **Baru Latino Restaurant** (2535 Alma Street, Westside, 604-222-9171, www. baru.ca). It also serves tapas.

Well recommended by a secretguides.com contributor is **Los Guerreros Mexican Foods** (3317 Kingsway, East Vancovuer, 604-451-7850). **Que Pasa Mexican Foods**, maker of excellent (and widely available) tortilla chips and other products, has done so well that it's decamped from Vancouver to a Richmond factory and deli (12031 No. 5 Road, Richmond, 604-241-8175, www.quepasafoods.com).

SECRET

LIBRARY

The new **Central Branch** of the **Vancouver Public Library** holds almost iconic status in this city, and it's worth checking out on that basis alone. The building stands, like some kind of Roman amphitheater, at 350 West Georgia Street (Downtown, 604-331-3600, www.vpl.ca).

Before 1995, the Central Branch was housed in what is now the Virgin Megastore at 788 Burrard Street. (This 1957 Modernist structure is highly acclaimed in design circles for what was, in the '50s, an unusually expansive glass façade, which made it inviting to passersby. When Virgin Records bought the building in the 1990s, it covered these windows with advertising, infuriating the design purists.)

By the mid-1980s, the city had outgrown the Burrard Street library, and city council held a competition to design its replacement. In a process that ended up involving the public in a kind of collective straw vote, Boston architect Moshe Safdie won out. The result was a $100-million building that, when it opened in 1995, was widely referred to as the Coliseum. The architectural community, and like-minded observers, made it clear they thought the design entirely unsuitable to the West Coast of Canada and a slap in the face to an honorable Vancouver tradition of Modernist buildings, reflected in the older library.

But the public had spoken, and over time the grumbling has died down. In fact, the library is hugely popular, if not architecturally, then for the many and excellent services it provides. It's also something of a social center for the city's large community of foreign students studying English. They shrewdly make the most of it.

No question, this library's light-flooded atrium, lined with eateries and shops and always busy, is impressive. The library itself is spacious, warm in ambiance, comfortable, and bright. As proof of its popularity, the VPL signs out eight million items — including CDs and videos — annually to 395,000 cardholders. The library is also remarkably well wired (given perennial complaints about lack of money), and provides up-to-date electronic resources and Internet access to library users.

On the top floor is the **Special Collections** division, with materials pertaining to the history of the city and province. In the basement is the **Children's Library**, which offers storytelling and other programs. Children's programs are also offered at most of the city's twenty branch libraries.

The one exception is the old-fashioned **Carnegie Reading Room** (401 Main Street, Downtown, 604-665-3010) — a small oasis in the otherwise heavily used and occasionally raucous Carnegie community center at Main and Hastings streets. In this century-old reading room, men and women who live in the cheap rooming houses and hotels of the Downtown Eastside and Chinatown have a rare place where they can sit and read, with others, in relative comfort and peace. The shelves hold 10,000 paperbacks, including lots of Westerns, mysteries and crime novels, Chinese-language books, and literacy materials.

One of the few complaints about the entire library system is the hours it keeps. The Central Branch closes Sundays in winter and for one week in August (although a new left-leaning city council has vowed to end that practice). Branch libraries close the day *after* a statutory holiday, as well as the holiday itself. The bottom line is that labor costs are incredibly high (and terms generous), and the city won't cough up more in operating costs for what is already a very big-ticket item.

SECRET

LICORICE

Check out **Dutch Girl Chocolates** (1002 Commercial Drive, East Vancouver, 604-251-3221) for its made-on-the-premises Belgian chocolates in flavors such as pistachio, champagne truffle, Advokaat (a Dutch brandy), and tiramisu. The store also sells cranberry bark, anise cubes, and a traditional Dutch wafer made with syrup. However, owner Alexandra Temple reports that people come especially for her 70 varieties of licorice ("I grew up on the stuff," she says of her childhood near Amsterdam), and a few samples confirm that this is an incredible, overlooked goodie. I came away with a tiny white-paper bag of what can be described, at best, as sugar-covered black pellets and was immediately hooked. Never again will I look at those plastic-wrapped strings that hang on the grocery counter as edible licorice. Here are the bona fide products of the California- and Mediterranean-grown *glycyrrhiza* ("the sweet root") — at once bitter, sweet, salty, pungent, and intoxicating. Also medicinal. Alexandra says the Dutch consume licorice for every ailment from colds to seasickness.

SECRET

LIONS GATE BRIDGE

Named for the two hump-like granite peaks that rise above the North Shore treeline, the **Lions Gate Bridge** was built over the First Narrows in 1938 by the Irish Guinness family, to better funnel traffic to West Vancouver, where they owned a big swath of potentially lucrative hillside known as the British Properties.

Designed by brilliant amateurs (Depression-era engineers, some of whom did not have university degrees) and built after 10 years of fierce politicking, the Lions Gate Bridge is a spectacular, triple-span suspension bridge with a ship's clearance of 200 feet. It remains a Vancouver icon.

In the late '90s, the provincial government dithered over replacing it with a tunnel or rebuilding it to last another half century or more. They chose the cheaper route, and the bridge underwent a two-year retrofit, involving regular all-night closures that saw high-wire steel workers crawling over the girders through the wee hours of wintry mornings.

The $125-million job went well over budget, but the procedure of lifting fifty-four separate 112-ton deck sections into place, each time in fifteen precision steps, was so well executed that the American Bridge Company and North Vancouver's Surespan expect to recover what financial losses they may have incurred in renowned — and similar — projects worldwide.

(For more on the history of the bridge, there's a great read in *Lions Gate*, by Dilia d'Acres and Donald Luxton, Talon Books.)

When the heavily used three-lane bridge fully reopened in 2002, perennial talk of putting a tunnel under Burrard Inlet resurfaced, this time between North Vancouver and the eastern part of downtown Vancouver. But by now the city was wearying of car-captive behavior. Public transit advocates and other critics loudly objected to building a structure that would only dump more suburban vehicles into the downtown peninsula.

SECRET

LIQUOR
❧

Many visitors find themselves flummoxed at best and, at worst, royally put out by their inability to buy booze in the nearest grocery store. Quick explanation: this province was heavily influenced by pioneer settlers who brought with them some serious Protestantism and temperance views. For decades, beer parlors in BC had no windows — to prevent the impressionable passerby from witnessing the debauchery that went on within.

The legacy lives on in the government's almost total monopoly on the sale of alcoholic beverages, and a related ability to generate staggering tax revenues. So, while there are a small number of independent wine stores around town, which were just recently permitted to sell hard liquor as well, the best places to shop are the BC **Liquor Stores** (www.bcliquorstores.com). These include a specialty store downtown, particularly for wine (1120 Alberni Street, 604-660-4572). Other downtown outlets include 1155 Bute Street, 604-660-4569 and in Yaletown (1108 Pacific Boulevard, 604-664-0118). The largest and best-stocked store is in South Vancouver (5555 Cambie Street, 604-660-9463). There's also a good one in West Vancouver (Park Royal North, 604-981-0011). Note: the above are the only government stores open Sundays and some statutory holidays.

If you need wine or spirits after hours, or are looking for a private wine shop that takes its products seriously, I suggest the **Marquis Wine Cellar** (1034 Davie Street, West End, 604-684-0445, www.marquis-wines.com). It hosts tastings and produces a bulletin with staff picks for "everyday drinking" or "cellar starters" (I'll take that 1999 *Ostertag Fronholz Riesling*, thank you).

An unapologetic booster of BC wines, I'll spare you my spiel. But if you're not already into Vintners' Quality Alliance (VQA) products, check out those at **Village VQA Wines** (3536 West 41st Avenue, Westside, 604-269-9433; Also 1811 West 1st Avenue, Kitsilano, 604-732-8827, www.villagevqawines.com). Both stock only VQA wines, made entirely from grapes grown in BC, and meet increasingly rigorous standards in both the field and production. A sister shop is **Edgemont Village Wines** (3050 Edgemont Boulevard, North Vancouver, 604-985-9463).

SECRET

LITERATURE

A single image lingers in my mind from a novel I read a decade ago: the book was one in a series of Willows and Parker mysteries by local writer **Laurence Gough**. I can still see the utter mayhem at a local gas station as several pumps exploded into a fiery hell and a couple of people flew through the plate-glass window of the adjoining 7-Eleven. All of the nine or ten books in this series of crime novels are set in Vancouver. Devoted readers — and there are legions — might want to suss out particular locations, although the gas station complex on Maple Street at Broadway has since been demolished by more benign means.

Karaoke Rap, for example, snags a corpse from the waters outside the fictional Coal Harbour Yacht Club. In *Killers,* a body is found floating in the now-whale-bereft pool in the Vancouver Aquarium in Stanley Park. Among the earliest and best known in the Gough series are *The Goldfish Bowl, Death on a No. 8 Hook,* and *Hot Shots.*

Stanley Park, by Vancouver novelist **Timothy Taylor**, was published in 2002 to considerable acclaim. Suffice it to say that it covers a lot of territory, from the perils of running a high-end restaurant in Vancouver to the dark secrets of its title subject. **Wayson Choy**'s *The Jade Peony* is a well-regarded tale of growing up in an immigrant family in the Chinatown of the 1930s and '40s. And **Malcolm Lowry**'s masterpiece *Under the Volcano* — the story of a single, tequila-soaked Day of the Dead in central Mexico — was written while Lowry lived in a $10-a-month shack at Dollarton on the north shore of Burrard Inlet.

S E C R E T
LODGING

Something you hear repeatedly is that top-notch Vancouver restaurants are far cheaper than their foreign counterparts. Ditto for accommodation. A recent survey by a US consulting firm showed that Vancouver is one of the cheapest destinations in the world when it comes to high-end hotels — an average of US$187, compared with US$430 and more for a similar room in London or New York.

New and decidedly trendy kids on the block include the **Loden Vancouver** (1177 Melville Street, Downtown, 604-669-5060, www.lodenvancouver.com). Very West Coast, very chic, the Loden is favorably located close to Coal Harbour, and walks along the seawall into Stanley Park. Another boutique hotel, the **moda hotel** (900 Seymour Street, Downtown, 604-683-4251, www.modahotel.ca) has taken shape in a 1908 building close to Granville Street and the downtown Arts and Entertainment District. It includes the celebrated uva wine bar, said to attract "the glitterati." An unbeatable location, coupled with relatively modest rates (for some guest rooms) will make the newly rebuilt **St. Regis Hotel** (602 Dunsmuir Street, Downtown, 604-681-1135 www.stregishotel.com) a winner. Also in the trendy, high-end category is the **Opus Hotel** (322 Davie Street, Yaletown, 604-642-6787, www.opushotel.com). This "sensuous sanctuary of contemporary design" will cost you, but the location is stellar. Another high-end option is the **Listel Vancouver Hotel** (1300 Robson Street, Downtown, 604-684-8461, www.thelistelhotel.com) Its art collection and chic décor set it apart.

For those with health issues, the **Fairmont Vancouver Airport** (Richmond, 604-207-5200, www.fairmont.com) offers an entire floor of hypoallergenic guest rooms. Adjacent to the international terminal, the hotel also offers facilities for a massage, swim, or workout between flights.

Is your budget a little more limited? A jewel of a hotel in a superb location is the diminutive **Buchan Hotel** (1906 Haro Street, West End, 604-685-5354, www.buchanhotel.com). It's within a few blocks of Stanley Park (and Lost Lagoon) and Denman Street, and not far from English Bay. Summer rates for a single (if you're willing to share a bathroom) begin at $90 and go to $149 for double occupancy.

I recommend the **Sylvia Hotel** (1154 Gilford Street, West End, 604-681-9321, www.sylviahotel.com) to friends or acquaintances who are looking for inexpensive accommodation. The brown-brick, creeper-covered Sylvia was built on English Bay in 1912 as an apartment building. It may lack the latest technology and doodads, but it's almost always fully booked: it's coveted for its rates, homey ambiance, bar and restaurant, views, and proximity to the beach, seawall, and Stanley Park.

Not only do patrons from around the world return again and again, but the 100-room hotel once had a cat that stayed — and stayed. That story is told in the successful children's book *Got to Go: The Cat Who Wouldn't Leave* and its sequel, *Mister Got to Go and Arnie*. Both books are available at the hotel. And the story continues. Sylvia Goldstein Ablowitz, who grew up on the beach and for whom the hotel was named by her developer father, died in Vancouver in 2002, at age 102.

Other inexpensive reliables include the YWCA hotel-residence (733 Beatty Street, Downtown, 604-895-5830, www.ywcahotel.com). The YW, with private and family rooms, with or without bath, is well located near the public library. According to a Japanese guest, it's "the best-kept secret in Vancouver." The modern YW fitness center is at 535 Hornby Street (Downtown, 604-895-5777, www. ywcahealthandfitness.com).

The **Vancouver International Hostel** at **Jericho Beach** (1515 Discovery Street, Westside, 604-224-3208, www. hihostels.ca) is a full-bore destination in its own right, nicely (if somewhat remotely) located on Burrard Inlet between Kitsilano and UBC. Amenities include private rooms, a rooftop patio, and licensed summer café. Getting there cheaply from downtown or Kitsilano means catching the #4 UBC bus. Take it along 4th Avenue to Northwest Marine Drive, then walk 400 yards northward to Discovery Street and a huge white building (a former air-force headquarters). HI also operates a hostel called **Vancouver Downtown** (1114 Burnaby Street, West End, 604-684-4565,). It's not far from Davie Street and English Bay. And **Vancouver Central** (1025 Granville Street, Downtown, 604-685-5335).

The **Greenbrier Hotel** (1393 Robson Street, Downtown, 604-683-4558, www.greenbrierhotel.com) isn't fancy, but it's conveniently located near Coal Harbour, and suitable for long stays (weekly rates are available). Similarly, the **Barclay Hotel** (1348 Robson Street, Downtown, 604-688-8850, www.barclayhotel.com) is moderately priced and boasts a good location.

I mention the **Del Mar Inn** (553 Hamilton Street, Downtown, 604-662-3282) because it's an odd case (this is by no means a recommendation). The owner of this budget walkup had a long dispute with BC Hydro over his slice of the city block now occupied by the provincial power giant. In short, he refused to sell and remains where Hydro does (or did) not want him. A neatly hand-printed sign says: "This property is not for sale and has not been sold."

Over the portico, in seven-inch bronze letters, are the words "Unlimited Growth Increases the Divide." This piece of listed public art was installed, says creator Kathryn Walter, both as a statement on globalization and as "a witness to the various power-plays that constitute normal business in the world of real estate development."

The well-located and nearby budget **Victorian Hotel** (514 Homer Street, Downtown, 604-681-6369, www.victorianhotel.ca) bills itself as a "heritage guest house."

Those who feel comfortable wandering off-the-well-heeled-path into a rougher neighborhood might try the nicely tarted-up **Patricia Hotel** (403 East Hastings Street, East Vancouver, 604-255-4301, www.budgetpathotel.bc.ca).

SECRET

LUXURY INTERIOR

Martha Sturdy launched her empire in Vancouver, and you can still find her chunky, bold trademark work — paintings, sculpture, functional art — at **Martha Sturdy Studio** (16 West 5th Avenue, Central Vancouver, 604-872-5205). Explains Sturdy: "Using casting resin, leather, steel and brass, I turn bold visions into tangible designs through working with my hands. My art is spontaneous as is my spirit. Each creation is unique, a handcrafted expression.".

Spiral Living (2207 Granville Street, Central Vancouver, 604-730-2566, www.spiralliving.com) imports gorgeous art carpets by Serge Lesage of France (reportedly the only retailer in North America to do so) and special orders for shipping. It also carries exclusive Provence-made and Italian housewares, both traditional and contemporary.

SECRET

MAGAZINES

Kent McKenzie and Dennis Topp run **Does your mother know? Magazines, etc.** (2139 West 4th Avenue, Kitsilano, 604-730-1110). Hanging in in a tough market, this smallish store carries a commendable range of hard-to-get Canadian, American and international magazines, including a number on the arts. Also a reliable stack of New York Times on Sunday, and some English dailies.

SECRET
MAPS AND GUIDES

Vancouver can boast a rags-to-major-map-publisher-riches story (subtitled "How to outmaneuver the pompous European cartographic establishment") in the form of Jack Joyce and his **International Travel Maps and Books** (www.itmb.com). Suffice it to say that this gregarious man overcame incredible odds to publish 200 professional and popular maps of the world's more remote countries, regions, and cities — and plans to map the entire planet by 2010. Whether you want up-to-date detail of the Queen Charlotte Islands, Hokkaido, Harare, or Kosovo, make your way to ITM and look over the fine collection now sold worldwide (much to Europe's chagrin). Unfortunately, you may have to go a little further afield to find the local outlet. International Travel Maps has moved just south of the city (12300 Bridgeport Road, Richmond, 604-273-1400).

Another resource for the travel enthusiast is **Wanderlust** (1929 West 4th Avenue, Kitsilano, 604-739-2182, www.wanderluststore.com). An all-round travel store with luggage, mosquito nets, pouches, and so forth, it particularly excels with its continent-by-continent selection of travel guides and literature. A smaller but well-stocked outlet is **The Travel Bug** (3065 West Broadway, Kitsilano, 604-737-1122, www.travelbugbooks.ca).

MARKETS

The **Granville Island Public Market** (www.granvilleisland.com) is no secret — indeed, the market and the island itself have recently overtaken all but Stanley Park as Vancouver's most popular tourist destination. You'd think this would warm the hearts of market merchants, most of whom have been making oodles of money as the market has grown in popularity since it opened in 1979. However, copious grumbling — also known as the politics of doing business — goes on non-stop behind the scenes.

Fact is, the public market, with fifty permanent tenants and a handful of itinerant farmers and artisan vendors, is the principal source of income for the federally operated Granville Island, so every decision made here has implications for businesses and institutions across the island. Market-related disputes have swirled around two issues: hours (it's now open daily to 7 p.m.); and the type of business (tourist-oriented or resident-oriented) that should be granted the rare available space.

Actually, the island's operator, Canada Mortgage and Housing Corporation, is pretty democratic. It periodically asks the public for their opinion and seems to listen. Expect to see, for example, a greater emphasis on farm-fresh produce and organic foods.

Germane to the hours debate is the growing competition from upscale health and luxury food markets around the city. The first newcomer was **Capers**, whose flagship store (now owned by Whole Foods) sits atop the hill in Kitsilano (2285 West 4th Avenue, Kitsilano, 604-739-6676, www.wholefoodsmarket.com). Hugely popular with the health-food crowd, Capers stocks an impressive range of organic produce, along with quality packaged goods, deli products, bulk foods, and exceptional breads and pastries. It also has stores in the West End (1675 Robson Street, 604-687-5288) and Central Vancouver(3277 Cambie Street, 604-909-2988).

Choices is another option (one of its several stores is located at 2627 West 16th Avenue, Kitsilano, 604-736-0009; others are at 1202 Richards Street, Yaletown, 604-633-2392 and 3493 Cambie Street, Central Vancouver, 604-875-0099, www.choicesmarkets.com). Capers and Choices have large sections devoted to health-related herbs and medicines.

At the luxury end of the spectrum is **Meinhardt Fine Foods** (3002 Granville Street, Central Vancouver, 604-732-4405; a large new store, with patio eatery, is at 3131 Arbutus Street, Kitsilano, 604-732-7900, www.meinhardt.com). The well-appointed premises stocks to-die-for foods ranging from imported condiments to fresh chocolate mousses.

But the ultimate market is **Urban Fare** (177 Davie Street, Downtown South, 604-975-7550, and 305 Bute Street, Downtown, 604-669-5831, www.urbanfare.com). This high-end food store, serving the burgeoning downtown peninsula, sells wondrous foods — from fruits, cheeses, meats, and pastries to imported spices, sweets, and condiments. Cut flowers, magazines, eccentric knickknacks — the stock goes on and on. But it's also a beautiful space architecturally, with a great casual Carvary restaurant that is a destination in its own right.

The largest year-round vegetable and fruit market in the city is the **Sunrise Market** (300 Powell Street, East Vancouver, 604-685-8019). It's a rough location, but not rough enough to deter a daily deluge of customers. Two sidewalks of stalls are loaded with fresh produce at good prices; the interior is one phantasmagoria of packaged foods from the Orient. Most of the stuff is still sitting in its shipping boxes — everything from satay marinade and small tins of pickled cabbage to giant sacks of Thai rice. Not to be overlooked is the wonderful, ornate metal work on the façade of this longtime business, which they call "Store No. 1" (No. 2 is on Westminster Highway in Richmond).

SECRET

MARTIAL ARTS

A large Asian population means plenty of outlets for the martial arts — Chinese, Japanese, Brazilian, whatever. You'll find judo, karate, kung fu, kick boxing, jujitsu, aikido, and more. The major provider of clothing and equipment, as well as information on the various arts and studios, is **Golden Arrow Martial Arts Supplies** (2234 East Hastings Street, East Vancouver, 604-254-6910, www.goldenarrow martialarts.com). If owner Gordon Arsenault doesn't know, he'll find out. He also serves the boxing community.

SECRET

MARTINIS

Clockwork Ohranj, Tequila Mockingbird, and Kamakuzi are the names of a few of the martinis you may find on the ever-evolving martini menu at **Delilah's** 70-seat restaurant and bar (1789 Comox Street, West End, 604-687-3424, www.delilahs.ca).

Two-ounce martinis are said to have *made* Delilah's, although the food is very good, too. Beverage managers and bartenders routinely turn up from around the us, even Puerto Rico and Europe, to study its infusions. The beverage people use foods such as apples, berries, citrus (lemon peel marinated for eighty days), and fresh vanilla beans for the bases; unusual blends such as papaya and habañero pepper for both sweetness and heat; and frosted glasses trimmed with cocoa powder for a classic chocolate martini, or a purple flower for the blueberry-infused Purple Haze.

I prefer a classic gin and vermouth martini that I associate with — romantic that I am — the era of, say, Noel Coward and Somerset Maugham. To complete this fantasy, I'll slip into the wood-paneled glory of the **Gerard Lounge** of the Sutton Place Hotel (845 Burrard Street, Downtown, 604-682-5511, www.vancouver.suttonplace.com), which is said to attract visiting celebrities.

Other great martini-making bars include 900 West at the Fairmont Hotel Vancouver (900 West Georgia Street), the Bacchus Lounge at the Wedgewood Hotel (845 Hornby Street), Cardero's Restaurant in Coal Harbour (1583 Coal Harbour Quay) and Chambar Restaurant (562 Beatty Street). Also Wild Rice Restaurant (117 West Pender Street) and the stunningly sited Lift Bar and Grill (333 Menchion Mews, Coal Harbour).

SECRET

MICROCLIMATE

When the westerly winds blow over the beaches and parks of seaside Vancouver, it can be pretty chilly. An option for a cool but sunny day is to escape to **Deer Lake Park** in South Burnaby, off Highway 1 at Canada Way. Deer Lake is an utterly placid body of water fed by dozens of small streams in a park crisscrossed with trails. In contrast to the coastal rainforest, this pocket of deciduous forest and marshy foreshore cooks in summer. It's a great place to picnic or lounge. Unfortunately, swimming is not advised.

However, aptly named **Silent Waters Boat Rentals** (also at Deer Lake, 604-667-2628), beyond the entrance to the Burnaby Village Museum, rents rowboats, pedalboats, canoes, and kayaks from March to October. High school athletes train here by boating, running, and cycling around the perimeter in triathlon-like succession.

SECRET

MOUNTAIN BIKING

On the densely wooded slopes of the North Shore mountains exists a somewhat anarchic society that most city dwellers know little about. These are the mountain bikers, and over the past decade they've acquired almost legendary status in cycling circles around the world for conquering (well, sometimes) this hopelessly rugged, rocky, and tree-strewn terrain.

They "huck" off ledges, and leap and scale rocky stream beds and slippery, rotten, fallen tree trunks — even planks, ladders, and teeter-totters they install themselves. Talk about masochism.

It's a culture, really, and you can explore it at the North Shore Mountain Biking Web site, **www.nsmb.com**. Meet the characters — predominantly male, but there's also a large female contingent that includes "The Dirty Girls" — through testimonials, aerial-act photos, videos, and lots of discussion of locations and gear for this extreme sport.

Deep Cove, a picturesque village on Indian Arm at the eastern end of North Vancouver, is home to the **Cove Bikes** (1389 Main Street, North Vancouver, 604-929-1918, www.covebike.com). Founded two decades ago, Cove claims to make bikes rugged enough to survive Indian Arm's particularly steep and unforgiving territory — or, in the shop's words, "the brutal, insane trails that the craziest of North Shore free-riders haul ass on." And while the Hummer-frame titanium model will set you back well over $1,000, the shop also builds somewhat less expensive models that will reportedly do the job.

Note: no culture is without its enemies — in this case, the hiking community. In the early days, some mountain bikers would "rip" (to put it nicely) past the hikers, jolting them out of their woodsy reveries. Today, the bikers mostly use their own paths and territory.

Further afield, the annual two-day mountain bike **Sea-to-Sky Trail Ride** runs from D'Arcy on Anderson Lake, south of Lillooet, down through Whistler and the Cheakamus Canyon to Squamish. This off-road ride entails a modest fee and includes food, festivities, and transportation for your pack. Organized by **Great Explorations** (604-730-1247, www.great-explorations.com), it happens in early July. The travel firm also organizes walking and cycling trips around Vancouver, year round.

SECRET

MUSEUMS

Somewhat obscurely located given its importance, the **Vancouver Maritime Museum** is found in Vanier Park (1905 Ogden Avenue, Kitsilano, 604-257-8300, www.vancouvermaritimemuseum.com) on Kits Point, east of Kitsilano Beach. Its star exhibit and a National Historic Site is the RCMP timber-hulled schooner *St. Roch*, the first vessel to make it through the ice-packed Northwest Passage from west to east. This wonderful boat, equipped as it was in the 1940s, is open to the public and ideal for children.

Also popular with families is a rebuilt '60s-era submarine capable of diving to 3,000 feet. NASA used this *Ben Franklin* on a month-long fully submerged voyage to study the effects of being cut off from the world for an extended period. The sub also made the first dive in search of the *Titanic*.

The museum also boasts the chronometer used by **Captain George Vancouver** to explore this coast between 1791 and 1795, and artifacts from the *Beaver*, the coast's first sidewheel steamer, which broke up off Stanley Park's Prospect Point in 1888. Below the museum complex lies **Heritage Harbour**, moorage to some of BC's finest old tugs and fishing boats. A suitably watery means to get to the museum is by passenger ferry, from a dock below the West End's Aquatic Centre or from Granville Island.

(The museum's presence at this expensive waterfront location has been controversial. In a nutshell, the mostly upscale neighbors in the area known as **Kits Point** don't much like the traffic drawn to the Maritime Museum and the adjacent Vancouver Museum. These well-organized residents hate the regular tour buses and have managed to limit the number that stop at the museums. In doing so, they've hurt both institutions, reducing their ability to mount major exhibits and make much-needed improvements. In recent years, the Maritime Museum has talked of moving to another North Vancouver waterfront location. Another fact: this entire waterfront was once a native Indian village and is still subject to land claims.)

Next door in Vanier Park sits the combined **Vancouver Museum** (1100 Chestnut Street, Kitsilano, 604-736-4431, www.vanmuseum. bc.ca) and **H.R. MacMillan Space Centre** (604-738-7827, www. hrmacmillanspacecentre.com). The latter includes a rooftop **Planetarium** — showing lively space- and astronomy-related laser shows, including those featuring the music of Pink Floyd — and the **Gordon MacMillan Southam Observatory**. (H.R. MacMillan, if you care, was a forester–turned–lumber baron who founded one of the province's largest logging companies.) The small observatory, with telescope, usually opens on clear weekend evenings in summer.

Directly beside the museum and space center — though skillfully wedged into the sloping landscape like some kind of ancient ruin — is the **City of Vancouver Archives** (1150 Chestnut Street, Kitsilano, 604-736-8561, www.vancouver.ca). Founded by a still-revered hoarder named Major Matthews, the archives is the keeper of city records and does an excellent job of it. Staff will also help you pursue genealogical records or photographs — more than half a million have been individually catalogued. A fine collection of historic photos hangs in the atrium, and history-related pamphlets and photo cards are available.

The crystals and precious metals that lit up a downtown museum that recently closed (the former Pacific Mineral Museum) have been incorporated into the new **Pacific Museum of the Earth**, at UBC's

Department of Earth and Ocean Sciences (6339 Stores Road, off West Mall, UBC, 604-822-6992, www.eos.ubc.ca). Suitable for children and adults, the museum highlights BC geology while looking at discoveries and advances in earth sciences worldwide. Expect to find anything from Irish Elk Antlers (really a specie of deer, petrified in peat) to a purple amethyst called geode — from South America, and more than seven feet tall. But the most popular attraction is the Lambeosaurus skeleton, the remains of a complete duckbilled dinosaur brought from fossil-rich Alberta to UBC in 1950.

Unabashedly old-fashioned, the **Vancouver Police Museum** (240 East Cordova Street, East Vancouver, 604-665-3346, www.vancouver policemuseum.ca) has been operating for more than a century. Apart from the overhead video cameras installed to discourage you from cracking open a glass case and stealing, say, a deadly butterfly knife, there's little that's modern here, and yet it has its, well, charm.

In what was once a coroner's courthouse you'll find dusty memorabilia, such as police badges, early bobby-style helmets, and lots of old photos of murdered officers, Depression-era strikes, and mounted squads (including portraits of horses).

More relevant, perhaps, are the displays of "street," "martial arts," and "prohibited" weapons, such as the "large-chain morning star" that hints at the caveman era. A criminal "chameleon" is the subject of a display that includes an impressive collection of phony ID used by a couple of rogues a few decades back; a drug-trade display looks at illicit paraphernalia common to Vancouver's streets. Dioramas recall famous Vancouver crimes of the past century. And an unsettling "forensic display" includes cross-sections of dissected body parts to demonstrate how coroners determine the cause of death.

No question it's an oddity, but if you're in search of the peculiar and (in its own way) wonderful, check out the **Exotic World Museum**, in the rear room of **Alexander Lamb's Wunderkammer Antiques** (3271 Main Street, East Vancouver, 604-876-8713). *Wunderkammer*, as Lamb explains it, refers to the small, unorganized collection of mementos that the well-traveled European aristocrat of the sixteenth and seventeenth centuries assembled in a room of his castle or manor house for the "wonderment and astonishment" of visitors.

Solidly in this tradition, a Vancouver couple named Harry and Barbara Morgan exhibited artifacts in their Exotic World Museum, just down Main Street. The items included postcards, photos, and other curios from the Morgans' thirty-five years of travel, mainly to primitive and tribal societies.

After the museum closed, Lamb bought the collection — a strange hodgepodge of amateurishly labeled and displayed stuff that's interesting, in part, for its devotion to collecting and lack of pretension — and asks only for a small donation to view it. Stop to talk with Lamb, a soft-spoken bohemian and seller of eccentric collectibles you'll find nowhere else — what he describes as "surrealist décor."

Vancouver has a Chinese population approaching half a million, and its story is told in a newish exhibit already declared a national cultural treasure. The **Walter and Madelaine Chung Collection** of 1,000 pieces of Canadian-Chinese history is in its own gallery on the second floor of UBC's Main Library (1956 Main Mall, 604-822-6375).

It includes a 13-foot-long replica of the *Empress of Asia* sailing ship; an exquisite opium-trade chest rescued from a Chinatown cellar; and 200 treasured Canadian Pacific posters that popularized global travel and the Canadian frontier in the early 1900s.

Growing up in his father's Victoria tailor shop, Chung was drawn to a poster of the pride of Canada's steamship fleet, the luxury *Empress of Asia*, which had brought his mother from China. In adulthood, the Vancouver heart surgeon collected 25,000 pieces dealing with Canadian Pacific's entire ship, rail, hotel, and telegraph network — said to have been, in its day, "the world's greatest travel system." But this collection also deals with the penniless Chinese who traveled to Canada in steerage to labor on the Canadian Pacific railway in the late 1800s. Definitely worth a visit.

A little-noticed gem, nestled into the eastern edge of the University Golf Course, is the BC **Golf Museum** (2545 Blanca Street, UBC, 604-222-4653, www.bcgolfmuseum.org). This modest collection, housed in the cottage-like clubhouse of 1931, is nicely curated and well maintained. It's the only provincial golf museum in Canada, at last report. Photos, books, trophies, news clippings, and video footage of the important moments in BC golf are featured. It also houses a good gift shop. But, most important, the entire museum is a charming expression of one aspect of earlier life in this city and province. Sport fans might also seek out the more extensive and hands-on BC **Sports Hall of Fame and Museum** in the BC Place Stadium (Gate A, Beatty Street, Downtown, 604-687-5520, www.bcsportshalloffame.com).

Another fine little museum is the **Hastings Mill Store Museum**. Built in 1865, and the oldest building in the city, it was barged to a waterfront park (1575 Alma Street, Kitsilano, 604-734-1212) in 1930. The museum originally served as the store for the Hastings Sawmill Company, which first logged what is now central Vancouver. (In 1865, Hastings bought land, timber, and water rights for much of the Lower Mainland as far as Howe Sound for the equivalent — in English sterling — of $244.04).

The **Roedde House Museum** (1415 Barclay Street, West End, 604-684-7940, www.roeddehouse.org) is a charming Queen Anne mansion designed in the early 1890s by one of the province's most renowned architects, Francis Rattenbury. Beautifully restored down to the stained glass and wallpaper and furnished with period pieces, this house shows what the finer West End houses were like at the turn of the last century, and how bookbinder Gustav Roedde and his family lived.

S E C R E T
NEON

Unbeknownst to many Vancouverites, this city once boasted the finest display of neon this side of New York. Well, that may be an exaggeration, but the city was definitely bright with "liquid light" — there were 18,000 neon signs in the Lower Mainland in the late 1950s, when the city fathers equated neon with sleaze and ordered them removed.

Most of the signs — made in Vancouver by a company that had won one of the early North American licenses for neon, and a number of unlicensed imitators — were dumped. But when local historians revived interest in neon in the late '90s, a few collections came out of boxes and basements.

The **Vancouver Museum** (1100 Chestnut Street, Kitsilano, 604-736-4431) owns some exceptional signs, some of which are on permanent exhibit in the 1950s gallery. They include a Silver Grill Café sign and window outline of dogwood flowers (the provincial flower); a Palm Ice Cream tabletop sign (1945); a garage parking sign (1955); and a sign that hung at a Loggers Employment Agency (1950).

Most impressively, you'll find here the Smilin' Buddha. This jolly,

laid-back figure once laughed and jiggled his massive belly above the entrance to an East Hastings Street cabaret of the same name (with the word CABARET is in bold oriental lettering). The decadent Buddha became a landmark. Jimi Hendrix played here in the 1960s. Later the club became a punk rock venue. When it closed in 1987, the Vancouver rock band 54-40, which had played its first gig here, bought the neon sign, made an album called Smilin' Buddha, and took the sign on the road with them. They finally donated it to the museum, which restored it to its full working order and blazing glory. Arguably the city's most remarkable neon remains the huge, vertical "Niagara" hotel sign, complete with plummeting falls. A few years ago, Ramada bought the hotel (435 West Pender Street) and replaced the Niagara name with its own, rendering the sign something of an absurdity.

A great piece of Art-Deco-style neon is the Vogue Theatre sign on Granville Street. And a fine piece of restored neon fronts **Dunn's Tailors** (480 Granville Street, Downtown). And just east of Main Street, the **Ovaltine Café** (251 East Hastings Street, next to a hotel whose sign reads "crackheads and junkies need not apply," East Vancouver) has long been presided over by a hanging swirl and inward-pointing arrow — perfect in scale and style.

A neon sign, said to cost an unspeakable amount, has gone up over the newest **Café Crepe** (874 Granville Street, Downtown, 604-806-0845). There is general rejoicing about this next step in the revival of the city's neon — and in a stylish font at that!

Serious neon seekers might check out www.vancouverneon.com.

SECRET

OUTLOOKS

Vancouver likes to think it's beautiful all over, but this is self-delusion. Parts of the city aren't very picturesque (the downtown peninsula, for the most part). However, you can get great views of mountain, sea, or river from a number of vistas, and a few locations will knock you out. For the North Shore Mountains try Stanley Park. Avoid crowded Prospect Point in favor of **Brockton Point**, at the northeastern end of the park, or make your way down to **Siwash Rock** on the seawall, west of the Lions Gate Bridge. For views of fjord-like Indian Arm, look northward from **Simon Fraser University**, a post-Modern mélange of Grecian and coastal architecture atop Burnaby Mountain.

For a Fraser River landscape that runs to lush, marshy habitat, visit **Fraser River Park** at West 75th Avenue and Angus Drive (South Vancouver); or, for river delta, make your way over one of the bridges to Richmond and **Iona Beach Regional Park** (for directions, see "Secret Hiking and Walking"). Button your jacket in any but August weather and walk out the long spit (really a sewage outlet). At the end, you'll feel that you're standing at the fulcrum of ocean, mountain, and river. Then look back at the south shore of the city, and marvel at the lifestyle it offers (modestly wealthy).

For a gander up Howe Sound toward the Tantalus and Garibaldi mountain ranges, position yourself on the cliff at the western end of the UBC campus (take care the waterlogged earth doesn't crumble underfoot).

But the ultimate views are from the North Shore mountains, including the **Cypress Lookout**, reachable by taking exit 8 from the Upper

Levels Highway in West Vancouver, and traveling up the switchback Cypress Bowl Road. From the outlook (on a clear day) you can see Mount Baker in Washington state, and the mountains of Vancouver Island to the distant west, with the city in the foreground.

SECRET

OYSTERS

There are few parts of the world better suited for imbibing what one food writer calls "zeitgeist on the half-shell" than the Pacific Northwest. Varied types of oysters are pulled from coves and estuaries from Vancouver Island to Puget Sound — each with their own degree of saltiness, sweetness, plumpness, or whatever other characteristics oysters boast.

And while oyster eaters might be excused for slipping across the border to Washington state for an evening at the expensive **Oyster Bar** (2578 Chuckanut Drive, Bow, Washington, 360-766-6185, www.theoysterbaronchuckanutdrive.com) or the slightly more modest **Oyster Creek Inn** (2190 Chuckanut Drive, Bow, Washington, 360-766-6179), Vancouver also shucks and serves up the gritty creatures by the millions.

At **Rodney's Oyster House** (1228 Hamilton Street, Yaletown, 604-609-0080), you can sidle up to the bar for whatever reason, but don't overlook the dozen or so varieties of oysters. You can also order clams, mussels, crab, or lobster in this popular eatery with a salty New England decor.

Joe Fortes (777 Thurlow Street, Downtown, 604-669-1940) is well loved for both its seafood and fashionable after-work crowd, and seasonally goes all out with oysters, as well as clams and mussels. As well as participating, with Rodney's, in oyster shucking competitions (world record: eighteen oysters in one minute and thirty-four seconds), Fortes serves up dishes the likes of baked oysters with Salt Spring Island goat cheese gratin. These are paired with an exceptional wine, of course (not cheap).

SECRET

PAPER
❖

"The last genuine stationery store in Vancouver," is how a literary friend describes **Avalon Stationery** (2033 West 4th Avenue, Kitsilano, 604-731-1535, www.avalonoffice.ca). The Avalon stocks gorgeous recycled papers in subtle colors, moleskin notebooks, must-have fountain pens and quality wood pencils, along with the conventional stuff.

Urban Source (3126 Main Street, East Vancouver, 604-875-1611, www.urbansource.bc.ca), which sells "alternative art materials," is heaven for those who love sheaves of great, leftover paper and oddments such as yet-to-be-folded little gold paper boxes, raffia, copper wire, glitter, film tins, and similar esoterica.

A different kind of source is a shop founded by artists — **Paper-Ya** (in the Net Loft, 1666 Johnston Street, Granville Island, 604-684-2531, www.paper-ya.com). Here, in the drawers of large wooden cabinets, repose sheets of luscious handmade paper in a variety of textures and colors, mostly from Thailand and India. The gallery-like store also stocks luxury leather-bound notebooks and albums, other literary-related items, and imported art cards.

Related is the **Vancouver Pen Shop** (512 West Hastings Street, Downtown, 604-681-1612). If you despair that the world of fountain pens and ink bottles is vanishing, or yearn for a futuristic writing implement that will place you ahead of the crowd, you'll feel quite satiated at this well-stocked emporium and Vancouver institution.

Those at the higher end of the social register should know about **Wintons Social Stationery** (2529 West Broadway, Kitsilano, 604-731-3949, www.wintons.ca). If you're looking for writing paper or wedding invitations that will hint at your good taste, wealth, or status, this is your shop (the stuff here is drop-dead gorgeous).

An eccentric Main Street bolthole run by two young women is **The Regional Assembly of Text** (3934 Main Street, East Vancouver, 604-877-2247, www.assemblyoftext.com). This is for anyone who loves all things paper, including intelligent greeting cards and stationery, and wooden boxes in which to store them.

S E C R E T

PARKS

The City of Vancouver lists 192 parks — although many are pocket parks, such as those created along Point Grey Road when the city manages to snap up vacant lots (in the expectation of eventually assembling a sizable portion of the south shore of Burrard Inlet).

While east-side political activists claim they're seriously short-changed in terms of per-capita green space by a series of since-jettisoned west-side-dominated city councils and parks boards, parks are pretty well distributed throughout the city.

The biggest is **Stanley Park**, at 1,000 acres (www.vancouver.ca/parks. The second largest park within city boundaries is **Pacific Spirit**, which takes in much of the forest at the end of the Point Grey peninsula, including Wreck Beach (Westside). It's actually a regional park, managed by Metro Vancouver (604-432-6200). (You can download maps for most regional parks, including a gargantuan one of Pacific Spirit, at www.metrovancouver.org.)

Pacific Spirit is definitely a jewel in the crown — with thirty-three crisscrossing trails totaling forty-five miles. There are twenty entrances connecting it with adjoining neighborhoods, and paths begin at major roads such as Marine Drive, Chancellor Boulevard, and West 16th Avenue. As to its character, Pacific Spirit is a fully regenerated forest.

The second largest park managed by the city, rather than the region, is **Everett Crowley**, built on a former garbage dump in South Vancouver. Residents of this Champlain Heights and Fraser River area play a variation of the east-side saw, grumbling that they live in a "forgotten" quadrant. However, if the crush of weekend walkers, many with dogs — for the moment, and controversially, this park is "off-leash" — is any indication, the public is not overlooking this area.

The intent is to keep Crowley au naturel. There are no directional signs on the 1.6-mile trail that loops through a mostly deciduous forest; newcomers, I'm told, are always asking how to get out. Somewhere in there are three lookouts over the Fraser River. The entrance is off Kerr Road, just north of Southeast Marine Drive.

If you're after access to the Fraser River, there are several attractive parks, including a smallish one southwest of Granville Street. But the best, for the time being, is the **Burnaby Fraser Foreshore Park** at

the south end of Burne Road off Southeast Marine Drive in Burnaby. Here, several miles of path follow the river (www.city.burnaby.bc.ca).

Long my favorite park (though Capilano Canyon is nudging up there) is **Lighthouse Park** in West Vancouver. Not that big — 185 acres with just under four miles of interconnecting trails — this park is nonetheless an airy showcase of old-growth fir and hemlock, framed by a spectacular, rocky shoreline. At its southernmost point stands the 1912 Point Atkinson lighthouse, one of the few remaining manned lighthouses in this region. The Marine Drive turnoff to the park is well marked.

North Vancouver, too, has great parks in provincial **Mount Seymour Park** and **Lynn Headwaters Regional Park**, a remote mountain park with trails to Grouse Mountain. There's also the voluptuous **Capilano River Regional Park** (see "Secret Trees"). **Cates Park**, off the Dollarton Highway near Indian Arm, is your all-round, family-oriented, picnic and boating destination.

The village of **Deep Cove** in North Vancouver — follow the Dollarton Highway eastward as far as it goes — has several parks, but it is such an exceptional place in its own right that the parks are incidental. Writers, artists, and film types live here; it often functions as a movie set. The village is, well, village-y; the ambiance modestly upscale and not overly hip; and the physical surroundings entirely, inescapably, coastal rainforest.

SECRET

PAULINE JOHNSON
❦

One of the odder people who influenced Vancouver was Pauline Johnson, born of an English mother and a three-quarter Mohawk father on an Ontario reserve in 1861.

As a girl, Johnson emerged as a gifted writer of poems and prose, and — more important — a commanding stage personality. For two decades, she rode the rails, disembarking in towns and cities to give riveting recitals of her Indian-related pieces, invariably dressed as the native princess she claimed to be.

She was a complex character: both fascinating and wayward. She is said to have sought the attention of men, manipulating them by appealing to their vanity. On the other hand, reports a biographer, women adored her because she appeared vulnerable and pure.

Late in her life, Johnson rented rooms in the 1100 block of Howe Street in an area that was then still largely residential, not far from her beloved English Bay and Stanley Park. Among her visitors was Chief Joe Capilano of the Squamish Indian band, who, though reportedly almost "wordless," would periodically relate one of the wondrous tales of his people.

Johnson wrote down these stories, reshaped them through her highly romantic imagination (and not to everyone's satisfaction), then saw the collection published in 1911 as *Legends of Vancouver*. Johnson died in her home in 1913. Her ashes are buried in a lovely grove of trees at Ferguson Point (Stanley Park, just north of The Teahouse Restaurant) and not far from Siwash Rock, the subject of one of the myths in the Capilano collection.

Ironically, it was the Vancouver chapter of the Women's Canadian Club — 750 wives of Vancouver's business elite of the day — who organized a solemn funeral cortège through the city. They later built this rough-hewn memorial, adorned with a not entirely successful carved profile of a youthful Johnson dressed as "Tekahionwake," the name of a great-grandfather she assumed as her own. Admirers were soon troubled by the fact that Pauline faces into the trees, rather than toward her beloved Siwash Rock. Further, her head is bound with braids, a style she never wore; and the piece doesn't really resemble her. Today, it remains as it was. On the other hand, there was always something a little skewed about Johnson's life, public and private, so this posthumous symbolism may be quite in keeping with it.

Her best-known collection of poems remains *Flint and Feather* (1912). Lost Lagoon, where she frequently paddled her canoe, was named for one of these poems.

SECRET

PHOTOGRAPHY

Presentation House (333 Chesterfield Avenue, North Vancouver, 604-986-1351, www.presentationhousegall.com) has quietly pioneered photography exhibition in this city, covering, over the years, everything from early Americana to the touring European avant-garde. I still have a black-and-white postcard reproduction, purchased a decade ago, of what looks like a Renaissance scholar's study shot by, I believe, a Czech photographer.

A member-run space that somehow survives on the goodwill of its volunteers is the **Exposure Gallery** (754 East Broadway, East Vancouver, 604-688-9501, www.exposuregallery.ca). Exhibits featuring the work of local photographers cover the gamut, from cutting-edge commercial to outstanding travel images.

Several colleges, public and private, offer part-time photography courses and programs. The oldest is **Langara College's Continuing Studies** program (100 West 49th Avenue, South Vancouver, 604-323-5322, www.langara.bc.ca). Another is **Focal Point Photography School** (4474 West 10th Avenue, Westside, 604-224-3636, www.focalpoint.bc.ca).

Really a wholesale outlet, but well trodden by serious amateurs as well as professionals for its bulk photo supplies and quality used lenses and cameras, is **Beau Photo Supplies** (1520 West 6th Avenue, Central Vancouver, 604-734-7771, www.beauphoto.com).

SECRET

PIG OUT

This may be unfair to diners who, in spite of the roll of paper towels ensconced on an upright peg on the table, behave perfectly decorously at **Memphis Blues Barbeque House** (1465 West Broadway, Central Vancouver, 604-738-6806, and 1342 Commercial Drive, east Vancouver, 604-215-2599, www.beauphoto.com) — I like to delude myself that I'm among them. But when you see the heaping trays of Louisiana-style meats, beans, and slaws making their way to a nearby table, and sneak a glance or three at the couple devouring the entire Memphis feast ("every meat plus all the fixins"), you'll agree that "pig out" is not out of whack. This is a small joint, so arrive early (or late).

Be mentally prepared to indulge in slabs o' ribs, brisket, chicken, and sausage — all "baaa-be-cue," authentically prepared on the licensed premises. But I almost forgot dessert! I recommend the southern peach cobbler — à la mode, of course.

SECRET
PIZZA

A friend let me in on the ground-shaking news that **Incendio Pizzeria** still uses a '70s-era brick oven at one of its locations (103 Columbia Street, Gastown, 604-688-8694, www.incendio.ca), and we checked it out. Indeed, the place has a Jefferson Airplane feel about it, and the pizzas are baked on an open fire. Incendio also makes Italian-style, no-additive, thin-crusted pizzas at 2118 Burrard Street (Central Vancouver, 604-736-2220), conveniently located next to 5th Avenue Cinemas.

Rich, thick pizzas — choices include spicy beef, blue cheese, sun-dried tomato, and sweet vegetarian — can be had by the whole or piece at the **Pizza Garden** (1042 Commercial Drive, East Vancouver, 604-255-1744). Thick-crusted Neapolitan and Sicilian-style pizzas are the specialty of **4 Brothers Pizza & Subs** (1417 Commercial Drive, East Vancouver, 604-252-8900, www.4brotherspizza.com).

An upscale option is the Alberta-based **Rocky Mountain Flatbread Company**, makers of what it claims is "real pizza" with natural ingredients (sometimes organic) and a clay wood-fired oven (1876 West 1st Avenue, Kitsilano, 604-730-0321, www.rockymountainflatbread. ca). The restaurant offers a dinner menu with pasta options and pizzas such as "fire roasted vegetables" or "bison," as well as a kids' menu with the likes of "simple pasta with cheese."

Nat's New York Pizzeria (2684 West Broadway, Kitsilano, 604-737-0707; and 1080 Denman Street, West End, 604-642-0777, www.natspizza.com) makes just about everyone's "best pizza" list.

Vancouver's own **Flying Wedge** chain flew right from the start, and with reason. It serves pizza that justifies the label *gourmet* — such as Szechuan chicken (with zucchini, snow peas, red peppers, cheddar, and sesame seeds) and spinach pesto (1935 Cornwall Avenue, Kitsilano, 604-732-8840; and 3499 Cambie Street, Central Vancouver, 604-874-8284; also Vancouver International Airport; the Central Library concourse; the Waterfront Centre Food Court on Cordova Street, Downtown; and 1059 Denman Street in the West End, www.flyingwedge.com).

SECRET

POT CULTURE
❀

The BC **Marijuana Party** headquarters and bookstore (307 West Hastings Street, Downtown, 604-682-1172, www.bcmarijuanaparty.com) functions as a political and social center for smokers, growers, and activists. Here, you can chat with "experts" on decriminalization advocacy in Canada and the US, and national drug policies around the world.

Don't be surprised to run into someone who ran on the Marijuana Party platform in a provincial election — the party fielded candidates in all seventy-nine ridings in a recent election and won 53,000 votes. You may run into party president Marc Emery — a repeat Vancouver mayoral candidate who promises to fire the entire police force and deliver heroin and cocaine to users' homes; publisher of *Cannabis Culture* magazine (www.cannabisculture.com); and claimant to the largest marijuana seed business in the world, dispensed through the Internet (that is if Emery hasn't yet been extradited to the U.S. apropos charges — controversial in Canada — arising from the seed-mailing business).

This storefront also functions as a tourist destination (unheralded by Tourism Vancouver). A wall map of the world holds color-headed pins representing travelers who've dropped by: to no one's surprise, the continental U.S. is chock-a-block with markers.

No doubt, those who work in the party center answer a trillion queries to the best of their ability; local pro-legalization celebrations and protests are also well promoted.

As well, the center acts as an anchor for pot-culture businesses. The cluster includes the **New Amsterdam Café** (301 West Hastings Street, 604-682-8955, Downtown, www.newamsterdamcafe.com), located in the space formerly occupied by the envelope-pushing Cannabis Café — until police and licensing officials closed it for drug violations. In 2004 the New Amsterdam narrowly escaped a massive fire that destroyed neighboring businesses, including "brother café" Blunt Bros. and costume and fetish-wear outfitter Cabbage and Kinx. The New Amsterdam, with its Dutch-like laid-back atmosphere, characterizes itself as "North America's premiere smoke-friendly café," although smoking tobacco is not permitted. It serves good, light food and sells pipes, bongs and other paraphernalia.

Papers (many varieties), pipes and blown-glass bongs, some by gifted Canadian artisans, are at **Puff Downtown** (upstairs in the mini-mall at 712 Robson Street, Downtown, 604-684-PUFF) and **Puff Uptown** (3255 Main Street, Eastside, 604-708-9804).

The B.C. Compassion Club Society (Commercial Drive, East Vancouver, 604-875-0448, www.thecompassionclub.org) lobbies on behalf of those who seek marijuana for medical reasons, and maintains a discreet location. Note that it is for members only, although you can visit by appointment.

SECRET

POUTINE

Belgian Fries (1885 Commercial Drive, East Vancouver, 604-253-4220) specializes in poutine. It's hard to believe that this Quebec-born concoction of French fries slathered in cheese curd and gravy could be popular on the West Coast, but, well, it just is. Belgian frites come in a paper cone with classic mayo, or toppings such as curry, chutney, Jamaican heat, garlic, and honey mustard. Also available is a Dutch treat known oddly as "war" — or maybe not so oddly, when you consider the stomach: it's a mix of peanut satay sauce, mayonnaise, and sweet onion on fries.

SECRET

PUBLIC ART

Hundreds of pieces of what is now called public art — from the outrageously dull to the playful and cryptic — are on display in public spaces around Vancouver. Those who want to explore this scene

in detail — locations, artists, dates, conceptual statements — can find the info on the **Public Art Registry** (www.vancouver.ca). The downtown peninsula alone has more than 100 listings, with many more throughout the city.

Among the more interesting sightings is *Four* (fiberglass) *Boats Stranded: Red and Yellow, Black and White, 2001*, which amounts to four seagoing vessels of radically different historical and racial origin perched on the roof of the Vancouver Art Gallery (750 Hornby Street) by artist Ken Lum. (You'll have to walk around this former courthouse to see all four of them). In the Robson Square plaza below sits an evocative bronze replica of a carving by noted Cape Dorset Inuit artist Abraham Etungat, titled *Bird of Spring*. And in the CIBC bank building at 586 Granville Street, an abstract mosaic wall mural by B.C. Binning perfectly expresses the optimism and creativity of Vancouver in the 1950s.

A traditional work is the *King Edward VII Fountain*, built in 1912 and recently hauled out of storage and reerected on the Hornby Street side of the Vancouver Art Gallery. The two granite lions sitting guard on the stairway on Georgia Street (which was an entrance when the building was a courthouse) were modeled after a pair in London's Trafalgar Square.

From here, things get a lot crazier. In a sandwich of a park at Hastings and Hornby streets, artist Daniel Laskarin has installed three wooden platforms with potted trees and wooden benches titled *Working Landscape, 1998*. You're unlikely to notice, but these platforms rotate (respectively) every one, eight, and 48 hours — commenting, presumably, on the unsavory rhythm of life in the surrounding business district.

Some of the most interesting and controversial public art is found in the recently redeveloped North False Creek and Downtown South areas, because the city has managed to extract significant sums from (albeit exceedingly flush) developers for public amenities.

Spectacular, if not obvious, is *Brush with Illumination*, a massive and elaborate steel, electronic, and solar-panel installation located sixty feet into False Creek, south of David Lam Park. Created by Buster Simpson, it's said to represent a giant calligraphy brush that, while taking environmental measurements of the tide and whatever, makes regular dips into the water — supposedly to be interpreted as paint or ink. Just to the east along the False Creek shoreline walk you'll find *Welcome to the Land of Light*. Woven into the guardrail is a series of phrases expressed in both English and the native Indian Chinook language — a comment on cross-cultural activity here in the creek.

Attracting more attention, for better or worse, is a giant steel sculpture called *Street Light* at the foot of Davie Street at Marinaside Crescent. A resident of one of the surrounding towers went to court in an unsuccessful effort to get it removed. He declared *Street Light* an ugly piece of trash that blocked his view and should be replaced by an ordinary garden plot. (No doubt he feared, with justification, that the public art committee might replace it with some kind of wild, postmodern landscaping.)

City officials will defend this piece to the hilt. I'm not entirely sure how it works; a camera that casts images onto its forty-foot beams sits in the center of the traffic circle (in what might have held daffodils and tulips, further infuriating our litigant). However, the result is that *Street Light* projects grainy images of False Creek in its industrial, railroading days when the position of the light is exactly right.

Even less popular is *GRANtable* on Beach Avenue between Hornby and Howe streets. This sixty-six-foot-long slab of concrete in the form of a dining table and end chairs takes up most of what otherwise would have been a nice park for picnicking or Frisbee-flying. State the artists: "Taking its cue from the grand rooms of neo-Classical architecture, *GRANtable* completes the axis of the existing grand stair by terminating the procession in a grand outdoor dining room." (Believe me, this is a prime case of "only in Vancouver.")

To restore your mood, you'll find a little whimsy in the 1300 block of Hornby Street, just north of Pacific Boulevard. *Footnotes* comprises ninety-four unpolished black granite paving stones engraved with a few evocative words or phrases. And *Collection* is a series of concrete and steel wedge-shaped receptacles designed to challenge the public perception of what constitutes "a public work." Is it a hip mailbox or garbage bin? It's kinda fun.

S E C R E T

PUNJABI MARKET

This vital market in South Vancouver, named for the ancestral region of the city's large Sikh population, is no tourist trap. Rather, it's a genuine ethnic market, extending along Main Street between East 48th Avenue and East 51st Avenue. Except for a Filipino food store, it's a solid and genuine bit of Little India, complete with sidewalk stalls and a fair amount of (not off-putting) disorder.

The market is known for its fabrics and six-yard saris — in fact, it's the largest fabric market in British Columbia. Stores range from the teeming **Guru Bazaar** (6529 Main Street, 604-327-4422), which carries imported fabrics and clothing from the tacky to the luxurious. It also stocks heaps of popular "mink blankets" — actually a polyester plush — on themes that run to (presumably) Indian tigers and African zebras.

Interspersed with the clothing, video, and music shops are jewelry stores selling cheap glitter by the truckload, or ultra-ornate necklaces and earrings of twenty-four-karat gold, suitable for a society wedding. For the finishing wedding touches, slip into **Bombay Bazaar** (6636 Main Street, 604-327-1261). It sells forehead bindis (stickers or liquid), turmeric skin cream, and henna for decorating the hands — along with stencil-like patterns to aid in the application.

The market is also a great place for food, the two principal restaurants being **All India Sweets & Restaurant** (6507 Main Street, 604-327-0891, www.allindiasweetsrestaurant.com) and **Himalaya Restaurant** (6587 Main Street, 604-324-6514). Both offer an inexpensive buffet of the usual curry dishes with naan (and other breads), samosas, and meat and vegetarian entrées — along with cabinets filled with honey-soaked pastries and other delicacies. The **Delhi Pan Centre** (210 East 50th Avenue, 604-327-0358) is a small take-out producing pan, an authentic Indian delicacy. Made with the betel nut of a particular palm and incorporating a white lime paste, the small folded packet is often eaten after a meal to refresh or anesthetize the palate. An acquired taste, perhaps.

The Punjabi Market reaches its zenith in April, when the Basakhi Day parade wends from the **Ross Street (Sikh) Temple** near Marine Drive through South Vancouver — home of thousands of Indo-Canadians — and wraps up in the market with speeches and celebrations. It's a colorful event dominated by would-be warriors wearing saffron robes and waving scimitar-like swords around for effect.

More than a decade ago, when the India-based Khalistan movement was lobbying for an independent Sikh state, the mood here was pretty uneasy. (The campaign had tangible support in Vancouver.) But things have calmed down considerably since then, with most Sikhs confining their religious politics to their homes and temples.

SECRET

RACCOONS

Don't be surprised to see an oddly lumbering trio or foursome of black-masked creatures coming your way. And don't be afraid. These little carnivorous mammals — actually, some grow to a fairly hefty size — are far more afraid of you than you are of them.

In spite of relentless urbanization, raccoons and (dare I add) skunks remain an important part of Vancouver's natural landscape. And while they generally live and breed in city parks and woods, they regularly amble into populated areas, presumably in search of food. I recently met up with a trio near Kitsilano Beach, at which point they scuttled up a tree. As soon as I passed, they clawed their way down again and wandered off.

If you've never met a raccoon, you'll know it instantly by its pointed muzzle, and gray to brownish fur — but particularly by the black band, surrounded by white, across its face.

SECRET

RAGS FOR HIPSTERS

In the past few years Gastown has enjoyed a renaissance, attracting avant-garde design shops and funky alternative fashion. They include **Komakino** (18 Water Street, Gastown, 604-618-1344, www.komakino.ca), with its dramatic black for men and women and refined yet avant-garde **Obakki** (322 Water Street, Gastown, 604-669-9727, www.obakki.com). **Dutil** (303 West Cordova Street, Gastown, 604-688-8892) stocks interesting denim from around the world.

While Main Street retains a different, less appealing grittiness, ultra-hip clothing stores can be found between the noodle houses and antique shops. Check out **Jonathan+Olivia** (2570 Main Street, Eastside, 604-637-6224, www.jonathanandolivia.com) for the work of "forward-looking" designers from around the world; **twigg & hottie** (3671 Main Street, Eastside, 604-879-6595, www.twiggandhottie.com), specializing hot Canadian designers for youngish women; and **Motherland Clothing Company** (2539 Main Street, Eastside, 604-876-3426, www.motherlandclothing.com), also showcasing indie Canadian designers. Trademark T-shirts are inspired by Japanese pop culture and Soviet propaganda.

Although modern Yaletown has evolved from a struggling fashion district into something of an interior-design mecca, some clothing stores remain, aimed at the young or the ultra-hip. They include **Global Atomic Designs** (1006 Mainland Street, Yaletown, 604-806-6223), which sells funky labels from Japan, the US, and the UK; and **Atomic Model** (1036 Mainland Street, Yaletown, 604-688-9989), with very different sources.

Lululemon Athletica (including 1146 Robson Street, Downtown, 604-681-3118 and 2113 West 4th Avenue, Kitsilano, 604-732-6111, www.lululemon.com) outfits the young-ish and trim with the latest in workout and sportswear. **The Block** (350 West Cordova Street, Downtown, 604-685-8885), nicely ensconced in an old inner-city building, sells interesting clothes for younger strutters.

SECRET

ROUGH AND SEEDY

While danger lurks everywhere — or nowhere, depending on your outlook — there are parts of Vancouver that call for some awareness, if not outright caution. First and foremost is the Downtown Eastside, the city's center until the early 1900s. By the middle of the century, it had become a refuge for out-of-work loggers and fishermen, poor immigrants, and the otherwise financially bereft. For decades, many (though by no means all) of its residents have drowned their sorrows in the hotel beer parlors that still proliferate along East Hastings Street. However, for the past twenty years or so, many Downtown Eastsiders — young and middle-aged — have turned to smoking and injecting cocaine and heroin. At last estimate, the area housed a good proportion of B.C.'s 15,000 addicts, many of whom are HIV-positive. Their turfs and trajectories, while not easily defined, are places in which to take care.

The social hub of the drug trade is the corner of Hastings and Main streets, specifically the sidewalks outside the city-run Carnegie community center (once the city's library and still housing a branch library) and west on Hastings. When the police show up, the regular sellers and users scatter. At any other time, you can stand on the porch of the Carnegie center, or along the south side of Hastings Street, and watch all kinds of substances changing hands in a pretty open manner, and desperados toking up, in any of a number of bizarre ways, on the spot.

Two blocks north, on the same side of Main Street, is the **Downtown Eastside Youth Activities Centre's Needle Exchange** (221 Main Street), which is responsible for freely dispensing, at last count, more than three million syringes annually. Continue past a police station on Main Street, at Cordova Street, and east on Cordova for a few blocks, and you'll come to **Oppenheimer Park**, an out-of-the-way oasis where many addicts hang out.

West from Main Street on Hastings Street, the scene is almost as bleak. And while city and provincial governments provide hundreds of clean and secure rooms and services for the ill and addicted, this stretch of Hastings — which includes the Portland Hotel, housing people with multiple afflictions — remains particularly rough.

While not the worst block in terms of drug-related activity, the 100 block of West Hastings Street, between Abbot and Cambie streets, with its unrelenting bank of abandoned buildings, is a clear sign of the economic devastation inflicted on the entire community.

There are other troublesome pockets: Blood Alley, a tarted-up cobblestone precinct north of Cordova and between Abbott and Carrall streets; the lanes of Chinatown, even into Strathcona; and the nighttime waterfront areas, including Portside Park at the north end of Main Street and eastward along Powell Street.

The drug culture has a presence elsewhere in the city, including Commercial Drive and the surrounding Grandview-Woodlands community. Much to the annoyance of left-wing organizations and marijuana activists, a community policing society moved into a former park-keeper's cottage in Grandview Park in the heart of The Drive — supposedly discouraging trafficking, and reducing the number of needles found in the park and surrounding residential gardens. At last report, business remains brisk at the corner of Commercial Drive and 6th Avenue; hold onto your possessions around the SkyTrain station, a few blocks to the south at Broadway.

Tired-looking Kingsway, a major thoroughfare that cuts through east Vancouver on the diagonal, attracts illegal gaming and other unsavory goings-on that very occasionally flare up into a stabbing or shootout. Some of the shabby eateries closet illegal VLTs (video lottery terminals) in their back rooms, and you play these at your risk. Though well supplied with Asian restaurants and clubs, Kingsway can be particularly gloomy at night.

SECRET

RUNNING

Given the seawall that extends around most of the central city waterfront, jogging and marathoning have become hugely popular. Serious joggers run in the pouring rain; some run to and from work. The Vancouver Board of Parks and Recreation's **Coal Harbour Community Centre** (480 Broughton Street, Downtown, 604-718-8222), is designed and programmed for people in pursuit of early morning or after-work exercise, with spacious locker rooms designed with joggers in mind.

The Bank of Montreal **Vancouver International Marathon** (604-

872-2928, www.bmovanmarathon.ca), held in early May, covers 26.2 miles through Stanley Park, False Creek, and Kitsilano. The 6.2-mile **Sun Run** — attracting almost 60,000 runners and walkers — takes place in late April. Its sponsor, the *Vancouver Sun*, likes to boast that it's the second largest "road race" in North America (www.sunrun.com).

S E C R E T

SEAFOOD

Go Fish, located directly above the fishing-fleet docks just west of Granville Island (1505 West 1st Avenue, Kitsilano, 604-730-5039), is a phenom. Open to the elements—year-round—this tiny eatery from Gord Martin, founder of the equally successful Bin restaurants (see Secret Bistros), is a modestly priced option for coastal seafood at its best. And from the outdoor patio (heated in winter), diners can contemplate their dinner's threatened sources. While a limited menu varies with the catch and season, you might find on it tempura-battered halibut (with chips and house-made tartar sauce), an utterly fresh salmon burger or imaginative tacos, sushi and soups. In summer, expect a lineup.

On the other hand, if you're flush, the decidedly upscale **Blue Water Café & Raw Bar** (1095 Hamilton Street, Yaletown, 604-688-8078, www.bluewatercafe.net) operates in a luscious brick-and-beam room, with several bars and a nice patio. Innovative dishes may include smoked wild sockeye salmon; cornmeal-crusted rockfish; or miso-marinated sablefish. Huge choice of wines.

The "Only" Café has seen it all. Opened in 1912, it has sadly seen its once-prime location (20 East Hastings Street, Downtown, 604-681-6546) evolve into the least desirable in the city, and it has no doubt changed hands a number of times. But this Arborite-counter and wooden-booth eatery still serves excellent, fresh seafood — from half-orders of fried oysters with chips and coleslaw, to sizable platters of halibut, snapper, ling-cod, or salmon (fried in lemon butter, if you wish). The value is exceptional — if you can overlook the spirals of barbed wire in the window and doorway.

SECRET

SEAWALL

This is a walking city — or at least a pedestrian-friendly one. This claim will infuriate some: there are a dozen or more pedestrian fatalities yearly, usually in dark, rainy conditions. But most drivers respect foot traffic to the degree that pedestrians habitually step into the intersection without looking left and right (not recommended). And unlike car-dependent suburbs such as North Vancouver, the city itself is well endowed with automatic pedestrian-crossing signals, some of which include an audio signal for people with vision problems.

But best of all — and unlike most American cities, where large swaths of the urban waterfront remain in private hands — Vancouver's waterfront is mostly publicly owned and accessible. The downtown peninsula, and the south shore of False Creek to Kitsilano, are almost entirely encircled with a **seawall** that is, well, the pride of the town.

An immigrant Scottish stonemason, Jimmy Cunningham, began building the Stanley Park portion in 1917. In 1931, as the parks board

took control of the park shoreline, he was named master stonemason. He oversaw the wall's granite-block construction well beyond his formal retirement in 1955. By that time, the Stanley Park seawall was three miles long. It was completed in 1980 — 5.5 miles around the entire park. After Cunningham died in 1963, his ashes were interred somewhere in the seawall.

Today, the seawall — which accommodates walkers, cyclists, inline skaters, and other non-motorized wheeled vehicles — continues east from English Bay and Sunset Beach around the north shore of False Creek. Portions of this section take the form of a suspended boardwalk. The seawall runs just beyond Science World at the creek's eastern end.

It then wends back westward through the newly developed 50-acre Millennium Water site. After accommodating athletes for the 2010 Winter Olympics, this will be a residential neighborhood. Architecturally designed waterfront pathways (and an artsy pedestrian bridge) pick up the seawall that continues past Granville Island to Vanier and Kitsilano Beach parks. Another newly completed portion of the seawall reconnects Canada Place, on the downtown waterfront, with inner Coal Harbour. This is a particularly attractive stretch, with developer-funded street furniture and interesting public art. In all, the seawall runs for more than 20 miles.

The seawall is not without its politics. Devoted walkers, cyclists, and particularly high-speed inline skaters periodically collide and clash (verbally at least). Parks board commissioners have talked about banning bikes or skaters, rejected the idea, and issued a press release or two to calm the waters. In the past few years, the parks board has started redirecting cyclists to alternate paths where space allows, and ordered all "wheeled-vehicle traffic" to take the seawall in a counter-clockwise direction (only in Canada would we obey!).

And as if that weren't enough official incursion, you can go to the parks board Web site (www.vancouver.ca, click on "parks and recreation") for "smelt-fishing restrictions." Dip-net fishing from the seawall is permitted for two six-week runs in early and late summer.

Anglers must have all the right buckets and so forth; keep well to the edge, and leave nothing behind. (Actually, this law isn't that bad. West Vancouver devoted an entire bylaw to its Dundarave Pier after neighbors complained of late-night fishing by outsiders, some of whom had left behind...fish guts!)

S E C R E T

S E X
❦

Womyn's Ware (896 Commercial Drive, East Vancouver, 604-254-2543, www.womynsware.com) portrays itself as the health-food equivalent of the sleazy sex-shop business — and, unlike its "XXX shop" compatriots, boldly advertises its wares through picture windows on, appropriately, the corner of The Drive and Venables Street. "Vibes, lubes, dills, and latex" are its mainstay, says its playful advertising. Its Web site chortles, "We're SOOOO famous."

Brandi's (595 Hornby Street, Downtown, 604-648-2000) is an upscale peeler hall of such popularity that it's spawned an offspring in the US. The likes of Marilyn Manson and Jason Priestley are said to hang out in this spacious room outfitted with poles, mirrors, steam (of various kinds), and scantily clad waitresses who serve hugely expensive drinks — watch your wallet, metaphorically speaking.

A couple of writer-editors do a Herculean job of assembling the *West Ender* (*WE*) every week, filling the giveaway (subtitled "Vancouver's Urban Weekly") with local news, entertainment, and attitude that arguably borders on "Secret Sex." But throw in several pages of ads for "adult services" and the paper lands squarely in this sex category. You can also find many of the same providers in the local *Telus Yellow Pages* under "Escort Services."

SECRET

SHELTER

Vancouver gets an average, irrefutable forty-six inches of rain a year. We adjust. And there are ways to deal with a downpour. A no-brainer is to carry an umbrella (you'd be surprised how many Vancouverites reject this option on the basis of some kind of enforced hardiness or other obscure principle). Another idea is to plan your urban walks with shelter in mind. You'll be glad to know that city bureaucrats intend to keep you somewhat dry. Builders and proprietors of sidewalk businesses are required or urged to include overhangs and awnings on their premises to provide a bit of cover during a heavy rainfall. Some of the newer city parks and pathways include roofed areas where walkers or cyclists can stop in a downpour. An example is the **Coal Harbour** area. There's a modern roofed refuge on the seawall just west of the Westin Bayshore hotel. Another has been built on the park that sits on top — yes, on the roof — of the Coal Harbour Community Centre.

Also, check out a longtime Vancouver institution, **The Umbrella Shop** (1106 West Broadway, Central Vancouver, 604-669-9444; also

1550 Anderson Street, Granville Island, 604-697-0919; and 526 West Pender Street, Downtown, 604-669-1707, www.umbrellashop.com). To custom order an umbrella in advance of a visit to the city (not a bad idea, and they make gorgeous ones), visit the store's Web site.

SECRET

SIGHTSEEING

Small aircraft flights over this coastal region are phenomenally popular. For numerous possibilities, visit **Tourism Vancouver's Info-Centre** (210–200 Burrard Street, Downtown, 604-683-2000, www.tourism vancouver.com). **West Coast Air** (604-606-6800, www.westcoastair.com) flies 18 times a day between Vancouver, Victoria and Nanaimo. It also runs tours to southern Vancouver, Whistler and up the typically coastal (and beautiful) Jervis Inlet, with a picnic below the waterfall at Chatterbox Falls. **Harbour Air Seaplanes** (604-274-1277, www.harbour-air.com) will fly you along the fjords and fishing villages of the Sunshine Coast, and into grizzly territory in the Khutzeymateen Valley of northern BC. **Pacific Spirit Tours** (604-803-1524, www.pacificspirittours.com) offers an overnight trip to Whistler, and tours of Vancouver Island and beyond.

SECRET

SINGLES BARS

A Yaletown denizen who should know claims that **Urban Fare** — the hip and enticing food emporium (177 Davie Street, Downtown South, 604-975-7550) — is the best singles bar in the city. Order a well-chosen wine by the glass (and, perhaps, a good, inexpensive meal), and sidle up to one of the working types in for a light lunch or for a post-office pickup (beverage-wise). Another option is **Joe Fortes** (777 Thurlow Street, Downtown, 604-669-1940, www.joefortes.ca), although you may have to burrow your way through the crush to the U-shaped bar.

A civilized spot is the **900 West Lounge** on the main floor of the Hotel Vancouver (900 West Georgia Street, Downtown, 604-684-3131). Lean up against the bar with, a glass of merlot or Campari and soda and you're sure to meet someone. But we're getting into fancy schmoozing here; a similar choice is the plush, lush **Bacchus Lounge** (845 Hornby Street, Downtown, 604-608-5319).

Racier sports bars include the omnivorous **Shark Club** (180 West Georgia Street, Downtown, 604-687-4275) and **Malone's** (608 West Pender Street, Downtown, 604-684-9977).

When you get a little older — say forty or fifty, or even sixty or seventy — you may feel at home at the ever-crowded jazz haunt called **Rossini's** (1525 Yew Street, Kitsilano, 604-737-8080).

Back at the younger end of the drinking spectrum, and with history of pushing the city bar-rules envelope and annoying the neighborhood, is **Elwood's** (3145 West Broadway, Kitsilano, 604-736-4301). This small slice of rusticana looks a bit like the galley of an 18th-century sailing ship (manned by rogues). I thought that martinis contained vermouth and gin or vodka, but Elwood's "Sicilian Kiss" blends Southern Comfort with amaretto — so there you go.

On a gentler note, newcomers to the city, or locals on the lookout for new faces, might try the **Billy Bishop Branch** of the 176 Canadian Legion (1407 Laburnum Street, just north of Cornwall Avenue, Kitsilano, 604-738-4142). It boasts, I'm told, a loyal, social crowd. The lounge at the **Yale Hotel** (1300 Granville Street, Downtown, 604-681-9253, www.theyale.ca) has been hosting blues and related musicians — and single people — for nigh on as long as this city has been going, and its devotees are legion. For a bit of true-blue — if shopworn — Vancouver, this is the place.

S E C R E T
SOUP AND SANDWICHES

Six hundred gallons of soup are consumed weekly on Granville Island, much of it from the **Stock Market** (northeast side of the Granville Island Public Market, 604-687-2433). The choice usually includes at least one with a fish and another with a vegetarian base. I like the cream vegetarian soups, always served with a fresh, grainy roll. But be sure to let the soup cool a little before even tasting; it comes straight from huge steel vats kept at a mean boil.

Terra Breads (2380 West 4th Avenue, Kitsilano, 604-736-1838) can do no wrong and is as well known for its hefty sandwiches as it is for its breads.

SECRET
SOUTH ASIAN

The Noodle Box (1847 West Fourth Avenue, Kitsilano, 604-734-1310, www.thenoodlebox.net) draws legions to West Fourth. A spicy peanut noodle box, teriyaki noodles, and Thai-style chow mein are among the dishes from this chic and budget restaurant and take-out. And it's licensed.

Hawkers Delight (4127 Main Street, East Vancouver, 604-709-8188) cooks up genuine Malaysian and Singaporean street food for take-out at a basic storefront. For inexpensive sit-down Singaporean dishes, there's popular **Kam's Place** (1043 Davie Street, West End, 604-669-3389). Kam's fiery green and red curries, tempered with coconut milk, come highly recommended. Also popular is the Malaysian **Pandan Leaf Restaurant** (2718 Main Street, East Vancouver, 604-876-3288).

Simply Thai (1211 Hamilton Street, Yaletown, 604-642-0123, www. simplythairestaurant.com) has done well with its fusion décor and similar cuisine. The **Urban Thai Bistro** (1119 Hamilton Street, Yaletown, 604-408-7788, www.thaihouse.com) is part of the **Thai House** chain (other outlets include 1116 Robson Street, Downtown, 683-3383; also 1766 West 7th Avenue, Kitsilano, 604-737-0088). Its signature dish is Horw Mok Maprao, a boneless chicken with red curry. **Sawasdee Thai Restaurant** (4250 Main Street, East Vancouver, 604-876-4030) is another option, as is the **Royal Thai Seafood Restaurant** (770 Bute Street, Downtown, 604-602-0603), known for its seafood, including local crab. The spiffy and minimalist **Tropika** (1128 Robson Street, Downtown, 604-737-6002 and 2975 Cambie Street, Central

Vancouver, 604-879-6002, www.tropika-canada.com) offers a large selection of Malaysian, Indonesian, and Thai dishes.

There are Indian restaurants all over town, and I've mentioned several in "Secret Punjabi Market." But for fusion food in a gorgeous space — with affluent boomers waiting, chai in hand, to be seated (no reservations) — head to **Vij's** (1480 West 11th Avenue, Central Vancouver, 604-736-6664, www.vijs.ca). An evolving menu will include the likes of grilled garlic mutton on skewers and "garnet yam and green chili dumplings in puréed onion and tomato curry," with cottage-style beers and well-selected wines by the glass.

Another Indian restaurant with a loyal following is **Akbar's Own** (1905 West Broadway, Kitsilano, 604-736-8180). City food writer James Barber likes its neighborliness, and its Kashmir and Mughlai-style dishes rich in cream and vegetables. Favorites include a lamb vindaloo served in a thick, spicy sauce "tempered with potatoes."

Clove (2054 Commercial Drive, East Vancouver, 604-255-5550) employs radical chic to transform Indian dishes into inexpensive fusion-type fare. This is the kind of place, with a pleasing if plain-Jane décor, that looks like it might be gone tomorrow, but isn't. Hope it's still there.

Vietnamese (particularly) and Cambodian restaurants are ubiquitous. Among the most popular is the **Phnom Penh Restaurant** (244 East Georgia Street, East Vancouver, 604-682-5777). Others along south Main Street with large, loyal clienteles include noodle-rich **Pho Hoang** (3388 Main Street, East Vancouver, 604-874-0832).

Several blocks of Cambie Street, south of West 16th Avenue, have accumulated good, inexpensive eateries, among them the Zagat-rated **Thai Away Home** (3315 Cambie Street, Central Vancouver, 604-873-8424; also 1206 Davie Street, West End, 604-682-8424).

SECRET

STARS

Many Vancouverites would like it known that this city has produced its fair share of entertainment talent over the past century. So the city-operated Civic Theatres has literally impressed the names and talents of some of the best known in a series of tablets on the downtown sidewalks of Granville Street around the Orpheum Theatre: it's aptly called the **Starwalk.** More than 100 people so honored to date include Bryan Adams (pop mega-star), Juliette (singer), and John Avison (conductor); also Larry Lillo (theater director), Ruth Nichol (actor), and Red Robinson and Vicki Gabereau (radio personalities).

Starwalk is part of the BC **Entertainment Hall of Fame** (www.vancouver.ca/theatres/starwalk), which continues with a **Starwall** outside the Orpheum Theatre's Granville Street entrance, bearing photos of other artists and performers. At the Seymour stage door (865 Seymour Street, Downtown), you'll find pix of international entertainers who, over time, have won the hearts of Vancouverites. These include Harry Belafonte, Mitzi Gaynor, Milton Berle, and Bob Hope. (All the hall's members can be found at www.city.vancouver.bc.ca, under "theatres.")

Volunteers of the Orpheum Theatre's own **Hall of Fame** (604-665-3050 for bookings) host public and group tours year round, when the theater's schedule permits. This masterpiece of oddball Spanish Baroque style was built in the late '20s by Seattle impresario Alexander Pantages for the fledgling talking-pictures circuit. The tour shows off the theater's long staircase corridor, the plush lobby of more stairways and balconies, and the deftly painted allegorical scene on the ceiling of the sumptuous 2,800-seat auditorium.

SECRET
STEAM AND SPAS

An underappreciated Vancouver institution is the **Hastings Steam & Sauna** (766 East Hastings Street, East Vancouver, 604-251-5455). Opened in 1926, it operates in the same wood-frame building it started out in. It's rustic and basic (and spic-and-span) — but what a deal. This genuine Finnish-style sauna caters to men, women, couples, and adults with children, in twelve private units (there's also a communal men's sauna). For $20 ($17 before 4 PM), you can spend ninety minutes in your own private, all-wood sauna — lying on the boards and pulling the chain that produces the robust steam that will propel you, again and again, to a cold shower. You have a choice of dry or wet steam (milder, and suitable for the novice). Throw on a little eucalyptus oil and the sauna acquires a woodsy, Scandinavian scent. Then collapse on a cot in your little rest-room and prepare to reenter the world. "Say it's a healing place — because it is," says a young Asian man working the desk. "Afterwards, you feel good inside. It's mentally relaxing."

Vancouver may seem an unlikely location for an authentic Middle Eastern hammam, or steam bath, but Canadian-born Surinder Bains Kassour coveted her own hammam after seeing one in Paris. With the support of her French-Algerian husband, she investigated hammams in the Middle East, and adapted their features to a privacy-conscious Western clientele at **Miraj** ("paradise") (1495 West Sixth Avenue, Central Vancouver, 604-733-5151, www.mirajhammam.com).

Miraj includes an arched, pillared, and tiled steam room, skilled practitioners offering an authentic treatment known as gommage, and a comfy lounge where well-steamed visitors are served tea and sweets.

While the hammam is aimed mainly at women, men are welcome one day a week.

Modern services don't come cheaply — indeed, the North American spa sector is inching toward movie box-office status when it comes to revenue. That said, city spas that may (or may not) inflict you with anything from a good pounding to acid infusions include **Beverly's Spa on Fourth** (2185 West 4th Avenue, Kitsilano, 604-732-4402, www.spaon4th.com) and **Spa at the Hotel Vancouver** (900 West Georgia Street, Downtown, 604-648-2909), operated by the **absolute spa group**.

Skoah Spa (1011 Hamilton Street, Yaletown, 604-642-0200, www.skoah.com) vows to entertain while exfoliating ("no whale music, bubbling cherubs or pretentious attitudes"). It will do up your face, feet, hands, or body with anything from apricot whipped-cream moisturizer to seaweed, in modern premises built into a former warehouse.

For details on spas at the airport, see "Secret Airport."

SECRET
STEVESTON

Drive south to Richmond (www.tourismrichmond.com) on Highway 99, then west on the Steveston Highway, and left at No. 1 Road to the village of Steveston — both a working town and a tourism center.

In the late 1800s, Steveston was one of the largest fishing ports in the world, with fifteeen canneries packing a total of 195,000 cases of salmon yearly. It was also home to a hard-living mixed-race community replete with gambling and opium dens, and bordellos.

During World War II the Japanese, and their fishing boats, were interned. Their story is told at the **Britannia Heritage Shipyard** (5180 Westwater Drive, Richmond, 604-718-8050, www.britannia-hss.ca); its Murakamis Visitor Centre is devoted to the story of a single family. Four of a dozen remaining Britannia shipyard buildings are also open to the public. In one, skilled boat builders restore old wooden working vessels.

The **Gulf of Georgia Cannery** (12138 4th Avenue, Richmond, 604-664-9009, www.gulfofgeorgiacannery.com), a National Historic Site operated by Parks Canada, is one of the few remaining 19th-century canneries on the coast. This is an experiential place, replete with the sounds of cascading tins and shouting laborers, where you can chill out in the Ice House (and smell the alternative to keeping fish ice cold). The cannery explains the various types of fishing boat that ply this coast, and the complexities of an industry that remains hugely political. It's open May through October.

The Coast Salish native Indians knew the point at Steveston, now **Garry Point Park,** as the "place of churning waters." This is the exposed shoreline of what can be a merciless Georgia Strait, so it's not inappropriate to find here a moving memorial to lost fishermen, in the form of a symbolic net-mending needle.

Traditionally, families would welcome their fishermen home by lighting fires on the beach; today, Garry Point is the only beach in the Lower Mainland where open fires are permitted. This makes it a great nighttime spot, but it's a year-round daytime mecca as well. On all but the worst winter days, people are here — walking, cycling, kayaking, and flying kites.

Steveston village has more than twenty restaurants, most serving seafood, including a couple of fish-and-chip places down on the docks. You can even buy, in season, catch right off the boats tied up at the wharves. Seasonal cruises depart from these docks. I recommend seeking out the rotund sea lions that bask on the offshore rocks in April and May.

SECRET
STRAVINSKY

Serious fans of the great Russian conductor **Igor Stravinsky** might be interested to know that the UBC **Library** (Main Library, 1956 Main Mall, UBC, 604-822-6375, www.library.ubc.ca) recently acquired the largest collection of Stravinskiana in Canada, among the top five collections in the world. Bequeathed by UBC-trained Dr. Colin Slim, an American music professor, the collection includes a signed edition of Stravinsky's ballet *Petroushka*, signed sketches of the *Divertimento* and *Les Noches*, and photos and portraits — 123 personal items in all. This is a treasured gift: Stravinsky conducted his music twice with the Vancouver Symphony Orchestra, in 1952 and 1965.

SECRET
SWEETS

Sweet Revenge (4160 Main Street, East Vancouver, 604-879-7933, www.sweetrevenge.ca) looks like an English afternoon teahouse but is really an evening patisserie that serves old-fashioned desserts to die for. Its seasonal signature delectables include a butter-and-chocolate cake with a bitter-chocolate coating and an Italian zuccotto — rich beyond rich.

Notte's Bon Ton Pastry and Confectionery (3150 West Broadway, Kitsilano, 604-681-3058, www.nottesbontonpastryconfec.super sites.ca) teeters out of the bakery category into sweets. Suffice it to say that its mocha-walnut torte, chocolate-almond pound cake, almond-apricot flan, and assortment of super-delicate cookies and old-style pastries are unadulterated decadence. For decades, the Bon Ton was a downtown institution with a loyal following; its new Kitsilano store and tearoom is just as nice.

An inviting space for late-night desserts and piano music is **Cheese-cake, Etc.** (2141 Granville Street, Central Vancouver, 604-734-7704, www.cheescakeetc.com). The confections come in various guises; "etc." stands for beverages such as hot cider and cappuccino. It's open every night of the year and can be busy.

S E C R E T

TAPAS

Given the speed with which restaurants and bars grab onto words like "bistro" and "tapas," I offer no guarantee you're getting the genuine item. But a wider trend to lighter eating makes smaller (and less expensive) dishes that can be civilly shared a sensible option.

Breads and patés, poutine and smoked bison carpaccio, are among the tapas-style plates at **Chill Winston** (3 Alexander Street, Gastown, 604-288-9575, www.chillwinston.com). This lounge-like restaurant includes a large patio at the cobblestone intersection of Alexander and Carrall streets, the hub of Gastown. On leafy Yew Street above

Kits beach nestles **Abigail's Party** (1685 Yew Street, Kitsilano, 604-739-4677, www.abigailsparty.ca). A popular dinner spot, tapas plates here might include slow-braised pork-belly sides, poutine (yet again, love that Quebeçois concoction) or Bourbon prawns. Utterly hot on the eatery scene is **Nu** (1661 Granville Street, Downtown South, 604-646-4668, www.whatisnu.com) under the Granville Street Bridge. Sample small plates: local albacore tuna tartare or oysters (with a lager shooter); chevre stuffed chicken wings; white bean and double smoked bacon soup. Another happening spot is **Habit Lounge** (2610 Main Street, East Vancouver, 604-877-8582, www.habitlounge.ca). Its motto is "make it a habit to share": suggested plates include yellow curried mussels, grilled lamb sirloin satay and the antipasti platter (with or without meat). Next door is **The Cascade Room** (604-709-8650, www.thecascade.ca). It's specialty is "cool cocktails; and it offers some pretty cool small (and large) plates too. For Japanese-style tapas, check out **Hapa Izakaya** (1516 Yew Street, Kitsilano, 604-738-4272; 1479 Robson Street, Downtown, 604-689-4272).

Some are already listed under "Secret Bistros," "Secret Al Fresco," and "Secret Latin American." Or the **Tapastree** (1829 Robson Street, Downtown, 604-606-4680, www.tapastree.ca). "Try the Ahi tuna with white and black sesame seeds, seared and served rare with hot Chinese mustard," advises a reliable food writer.

Film industry types are said to hang out at **The Alibi Room** (157 Alexander Street, Gastown, 604-623-3383, www.alibi.ca). Maybe they're drawn by the crab and corn cakes, or the yucca and yam chips with chipotle mayonnaise — as well as each other, of course. Or its "modern tavern" ambiance.

A downtown reliable, and open into the early morning hours, is **La Bodega Restaurante & Tapas Bar** (1277 Howe Street, Downtown, 604-684-8814, www.labodegavancouver.com).

S E C R E T

TEA
✤

Interestingly, what are arguably Vancouver's most influential immigrant groups — the English, Chinese, and Indians — come from big tea cultures. It stands to reason, then, that tea drinking is big on the coast, although tea comes in some wildly diverse guises.

A perfect English afternoon high tea can be had at the **Secret Garden Tea Company** (5559 West Boulevard, Kerrisdale Village, Westside, 604-261-3070, www.secretgardentea.com). Save space for those yummy little crustless sandwiches and old-fashioned pastries.

In a different vein, there's **T, the Tearoom** (1568 West Broadway, Central Vancouver, 604-730-8390, www.tealeaves.com). This attractive space on a minimalist Asian theme serves 200 teas, many of which are sold through a Vancouver-based parent company to high-end hotels and restaurants around the continent. Here they serve a variety of oolongs, green teas, infusions, and traditional black blends. **Ten Ren Tea and Ginseng Co.** (550 Main Street, Chinatown, 604-684-1566, www.tenren.com) and **Ten Lee** (500 Main Street, Chinatown, 604-689-7598), run by the same people, promote the art of making Chinese tea (correct quantity, temperature, pot, and steeping). The Taiwanese-based importer sells green, red, white, yellow, and black teas grown in the mountains of Taiwan and China.

O-Cha Tea Bar (1116 Homer Street, Yaletown, 604-633-3929, www.o-chateabar.com), in a converted warehouse, stocks sixty varieties of loose tea. Among them is the South African "rooibos," said to do all kinds of good things to your body. The lemon rooibos is subtle and soothing.

Murchie's Tea & Coffee (825 West Pender Street, Downtown, 604-

669-0783; and Oakridge Centre, South Vancouver, 604-872-6930, www.murchies.com) remains a city institution. On Pender, at least, where I occasionally fill an order of my late and beloved Aunt Kay's own blend (they hold on to personal recipes for an eternity), the tea blenders are friendly and well informed.

SECRET

TENNIS

Tennis buffs might want to check out the UBC **Coast Indoor Tennis Centre** (6160 Thunderbird Boulevard, UBC, 604-822-2505, www.tennis.ubc.ca).

SECRET

THEATER

You can't go wrong — well, don't hold me to that — by checking out the happenings at the **Vancouver East Cultural Centre** (1895 Venables Street, East Vancouver, 604-254-9578, www.thecultch.com). I've seen some awful touring theater at this woodsy former church, but some excellent shows, too. Let it be known, though, that The Cultch, as it's called, is an east-side icon — or, in its own words, one of Vancouver's "cultural treasures." Many performers and shows — music, dance, theater and family fare — have been launched here, and it continues to host a wide array of the adventurous and avant-garde.

At the **Jericho Arts Centre** (1675 Discovery Street, off Northwest Marine Drive, Westside, www.jerichoartscentre.com), you'll find the **United Players** (604-224-8007, www.unitedplayers.com), a long-time company employing emerging and professional actors, directors, and technicians in frequently good, challenging productions. Thank tireless artistic director Andrée Karas, who may well be standing by the door when you step from the hall into the (occasionally) starlit setting of Jericho Beach Park and English Bay.

Performance Works is an artsy, minimalist space — all wood beams and corrugated iron (1218 Cartwright Street, Granville Island, 604-687-3020). Just about everything happens here during a year, from off-the-wall opera to progressive jazz.

The Firehall Arts Centre (280 East Cordova Street, East Vancouver, 604-689-0926, www.firehallartscentre.ca), in a 1906 heritage fire hall, includes a small proscenium theater and upstairs bar, though it's all pretty basic. It mounts contemporary theater and dance from across Canada — always topical, sometimes controversial. The **Havana** (1212 Commercial Drive, East Vancouver, 604-253-9119, www.havanarestaurant.ca) is a sixty-seat theater adjoining the restaurant of the same name. Very Commercial Drive.

A consistent deliverer of intelligent, avant-garde theater is **Studio 58** at Langara College (100 West 49th Avenue, South Vancouver, 604-323-5227, www.langara.bc.ca/studio58). Although it's closed during summer, for the remainder of the year drama students do exceptional work under hand-picked directors.

Unbeknownst to just about everybody, the 3,000-seat **Queen Elizabeth Theatre**, one of three city-owned theaters (the others are the Vancouver Playhouse in the same complex, and Orpheum Theatre, all at www.vancouver.ca/theatres), won a 2001 Governor General's Award for architecture and interior design for three "salons." These glitzy rooms, nestled between the two theaters, are intended for corporate gatherings but can be rented by anyone. Treat your friends — the rents are modest (Vancouver Civic Theatres, 649 Cambie Street, Downtown, 604-665-3050).

Pacific Theatre, in the Holy Trinity Anglican Church complex (1440 West 12th Avenue, Central Vancouver, 604-731-5518, www.holytrinityvancouver.org) was founded by a small group of professional actors. Its full season of plays is inclusive and broadly spiritual in nature.

This is a bare beginning: for more on theater and other arts-related happenings, contact the **Alliance for Arts and Culture** (604-681-3535, www.allianceforarts.com) or visit www.ticketstonight.ca.

SECRET

THEATER IN PARKS

Theatre Under the Stars (Malkin Bowl, Stanley Park, www.tuts.ca) has been staging popular musicals in Stanley Park forever — just about every longtime Vancouverite has seen a production of the likes of *Gentlemen Prefer Blondes, South Pacific* or *Annie Get Your Gun*. These years, TUTS runs two semi-professional productions during July and August (sky permitting) in its 2,000-seat outdoor Malkin Bowl. (Word is, the old structure may face a wrecking ball one of these days, so get there soon.) Take your blanket and umbrella; if it's nice, people picnic beforehand on the lawn.

The **Bard on the Beach Shakespeare Festival** (604-739-0559, www.bardonthebeach.org) stages two Shakespearean plays in its 520-seat main-stage tent in Kitsilano's Vanier Park, June through September. It remains, year after year, so successful that it can't fall into anyone's "secret" realm. But what's not common knowledge is that the company also mounts lesser-known masterpieces — "rich nuts of the canon that other theaters don't do," according to publicist Diana King — in its intimate 240-seat **Douglas Campbell Studio Stage**. One year, it was *Cymbeline*; another, *Two Gentlemen of Verona*. Each is done in a classical style, under the direction of Bard on the Beach founder Christopher Gaze.

A funny old showplace is the **Kits Showboat** (in the bleachers above the Kitsilano Pool in the 2200 block of Cornwall Avenue, 604-734-7332, www.kitsilanoshowboat.com). On weekday evenings in summer, weather permitting, amateurs of all ages do their thing here. It's as much a cultural phenomenon as entertainment, but it's a great spot and free.

SECRET

TIME

❖

A blow to the illusion that Vancouver is some kind of laid-back metropolis where time doesn't matter is struck by its modest collection of oddball timepieces. Arguably the most attractive is the 1905 wooden-movement **Birks Clock** that stands outside the upscale downtown jewelry store at Hastings and Granville streets. Oddly, this icon was originally erected across the street on the same corner. But Henry Birks moved it up to the southeast corner of Georgia and

Granville streets in 1912, where it remained until Birks moved north again in 1994. (The demolition of the terra-cotta Birks building on Georgia Street in 1974 remains a sore point with heritage activists and lots of ordinary city-watchers, but that's another story).

Another historical timepiece is the **Nine o'Clock Gun** — actually, a cannon that goes off precisely at nine PM and can be heard, or felt, through much of northwest Vancouver. There are several theories about how the cannon got where it is, none definitive. The copper, tin, and antimony gun sits in a hut near the water's edge just east of Brockton Oval in Stanley Park. It has been fired nightly since 1894, almost without interruption (the longest silent period was during World War II).

A time marker more likely to shatter your nerves is the set of ten cast-aluminum horns that goes off atop Canada Place daily at noon. Blasting out the first four notes of "O Canada," the **Noon Horn** appeals to latent nationalism, I guess. A sensible effort in the mid-1990s to remove the assemblage from its former perch atop the BC Hydro building on Nelson Street (as the building was about to be transformed into a residential complex), and pack it away forever, brought howls of protest. As some compensation, the horns now face northward, blasting their unappealing sound over Burrard Inlet.

I've said I wasn't going to mention it, but I've seen the **Gastown Steam Clock** listed among the "ten least-appealing tourist attractions" in Vancouver, and it may be worth checking out on that basis alone. When you find it in Gastown at the corner of Water and Cambie streets, you're likely to encounter a phalanx of tourists photographing one another standing in front of it as it gurgles, creaks, and puffs (every fifteen minutes). Adding to its popularity is the fact that the cast-bronze clock, built in 1977 by a local clockmaker, somewhat resembles a miniature Big Ben. Ah, the drawing power of celebrity.

If you're in the historic district of Mount Pleasant, you can't miss the landmark **Heritage Hall** (3102 Main Street, East Vancouver), built in 1916 as a postal station, and its decorative Beaux Arts tower and clock, made in Whitchurch, England. An oddity, it ticks forty-eight times every minute; a two-ton bronze bell sounds every hour from 9 AM to 9 PM. Members of the BC chapter of the National Association of Clock and Watchmakers wind it once a week.

SECRET

TOILETS

A few years back I (almost literally) stumbled upon the public toilets directly underneath Vancouver's most trouble-prone intersection — **Main Street** and **Hastings Street**, Downtown — and their redoubtable caretakers, Jim and Julie Scott. To telescope a harrowing tale, this middle-aged couple turfed the sex-and-drug trade from the century-old underground men's and women's toilets, and returned them to public use. And believe me, dealing with the females in particular (backed, of course, by their pimps) was no easy task. Julie is a soft-spoken, no-nonsense native woman from northern Alberta. In a cubicle behind the toilets, decorated with photos of her children and grandkids, she reads paperback novels — her other eye on a mirror. Jim is a genial, worldly soul who hands out far too many cigarettes to pleading drifters, and handles difficult situations with incredible calm.

Not only do the Scotts battle frequent violence and unspeakable messes, they face head-on the fierce and often irrational politics at this drug-trafficking central, including those of the adjacent city-run Carnegie community center.

The Scotts also oversee the only other historic public washrooms on the peninsula in **Victory Square**, on Hamilton Street, at Hastings Street (Downtown). These conveniences have something of an Art Deco appearance, and less traffic and turmoil.

The Vancouver Archives has architectural designs for other public toilets proposed at a time when there were no other public options. It's a shame that those that were built, several with elaborate wrought-iron entrances, have long vanished. Good thing there are alternatives. Among accessible downtown washrooms are those in the public foyer of the **Vancouver Art Gallery** (750 Hornby Street); **The Bay** department store (Granville Street, at Georgia Street); and the **Vancouver Public Library** (350 West Georgia Street). The Broadway corridor can feel pretty toilet-unfriendly if you're in a crunch, but no one blinks an eye if you slip into the **Holiday Inn** (711 West Broadway, Central Vancouver): you'll find the facilities on your right, down the steps toward the lounge.

The city has installed some automated self-cleaning toilets in the Downtown Eastside and Granville Street entertainment district. They are open 24/7 and free. Despite some vandalism, seems they're deemed a success.

SECRET

TRAINS

Railways helped build Vancouver — **Engine 374**, which pulled the first transcontinental service into the city on May 23, 1887, sits in a glass pavilion at the Roundhouse (Davie Street and Pacific Boulevard, Downtown South) — and continue to play an important role in this province. Via Rail's latter-day transcontinental service departs from **Pacific Central Station** (1150 Station Street, Central Vancouver, 800-561-8630, www.viarail.ca).

The **Stanley Park Miniature Railway** (604-257-8531, www.vancouver.ca/parks), pulled by an exact replica of Engine 374, keeps chugging on. It runs a fifteen-minute summer train through the towering firs and cedars; a spooky Halloween train (much of October); and a glorious Christmas-time trip full of fun and twinkle (through December). The railway starts near the Stanley Park Dining Pavilion and picnic area off Pipeline Road. It's pretty inexpensive.

Still on a tourist theme, by 2010, a small, tourist-oriented **Heritage Streetcar** will run along a track south of False Creek between the Canada Line station at Cambie Street and 2nd Avenue and Granville Island. A longer-term goal is to revive a long-abandoned streetcar system that once ran throughout the city. While this is going to take some creative financing, the city has plans to extend this tourist-oriented streetcar service down through Chinatown, with branch lines to the north shore of False Creek and across the inner city to Coal Harbour.

A more genuine rail service — although serious railway types argue that the city's ALRT (automated light rapid transit) system is a bloody poor excuse for a train — is the **SkyTrain** system (info, 604-953-3333, www.translink.bc.ca). The original line connects North Surrey, New Westminster, Burnaby, and East Vancouver with the downtown peninsula. The Millennium Line takes a slightly different route from New Westminster, through Burnaby, and into Vancouver, terminating at a station west of Broadway and Commercial Drive. Take the SkyTrain. It offers a backyard view of Vancouver and great panoramas of the eastern suburbs and Fraser River.

The **West Coast Express** is a spiffy commuter train that connects communities on the north shore of the Fraser River with downtown Vancouver. Unfortunately, it runs into the city in the morning and out in the late afternoon — not very accommodating to casual travelers. But, hey, it's a train, and a pretty comfortable one at that. When the taxpayers of Vancouver learned that the massively subsidized service includes laptop plug-ins and cappuccino service, the envy (and annoyance) was palpable. Suburbanites flocked to it, understandably. It departs from the Waterfront Station on West Cordova Street (Downtown, 604-488-8906, www.westcoastexpress.com.)

The big news is the opening of the **Canada Line** for the 2010 Winter Olympics (www.canadaline.ca). Of course, the construction process was controversial and painful, but we finally have a rapid train to and from the airport. The costly mega-system, mostly underground and with 16 stations, runs from Waterfront Station, along the Cambie Street corridor, to suburban Richmond and YVR.

S E C R E T

TREES

It's pretty hard to talk about Vancouver without mentioning trees (there are 100,000 publicly owned *street* trees alone). Some forestry experts believe that this wet, temperate climate has produced the largest evergreens anywhere in the world, and the legacy lives. There are people in this city so tree-obsessed that when anyone appears anywhere near a tree with a chainsaw, they immediately phone a city official or newspaper reporter as if someone is about to commit a murder.

There are homeowners who love to live under a perennial canopy of gloomy conifers that drip endless water onto the roof, gutters, and swampy soil. Then there are others who argue the need for more sunlight and would gladly clear-cut their entire property, given the opportunity — and occasionally do. City council debates and public meetings over tree-cutting policies (and fines) can, therefore, turn decidedly nasty.

Almost all the old growth that covered Vancouver is gone, although a few small stands remain — those trees in **Stanley Park** deemed too large to cut by those who logged the 1,000 acres in the mid-to-late 1800s. You'll find "monument" Douglas firs in an original grove on the Tunnel Trail off Pipeline Road, between the Rose Garden and Stanley Park Drive; and towering firs and western red cedars along the Third Beach Trail.

In 2006, a storm of near hurricane force took down more than 1,000 trees (the event was treated by some as a civic disaster), and the damage remains obvious. Large pockets, once dense with green, are now thin and patchy, and some fallen conifers have yet to be removed.

The damage was particularly severe around Prospect Point. Widespread rockslides closed the seawall for many months.

In recent years, officials have been trying to tell those Vancouverites who will listen that giant, aging trees are unsuitable for a densely populated urban area, and parks officials now plant mostly smaller ornamental trees, many of which blossom in spring. As a result, two of the nicest months in Vancouver are April and May, when the flowering varieties produce a pink or white gossamer scene along many streets (**Southwest Marine Drive** in South Vancouver is among the most spectacular).

In Stanley Park, the entire landscape around the tennis courts at the park's southern entrance (Beach Avenue) is said to have a priceless collection of ornamentals. Mature tree-like azaleas and rhododendrons, weeping beech, and flowering magnolias nestle under towering evergreens.

And there are great tree clusters around the city: **Cambie Boulevard** holds a series of giant sequoia, **West 10th Avenue** between Blenheim and Alma streets is a grand treed promenade; on **Kitsilano Beach**, massive weeping willows perform when it blows; and **Queen Elizabeth Park** and the **VanDusen Botanical Garden** (see "Secret Gardens") have a raft of exceptional trees and species.

Worth seeking out is the **Riverview Arboretum** (off the Lougheed Highway in Coquitlam, 604-290-9910, www.thcs.org), planted in the early 1900s on the grounds of what has long been an institution for the mentally ill, now Riverview Hospital. Modeled on England's Kew Gardens, this is a rolling hillside of massive, shapely trees in their glorious maturity.

If ornamental trees just won't do and you still want to see old growth, you'll have to venture onto the North Shore, where some record-break-ing giants are said to exist. Among them are western red cedars more than sixteen feet in diameter, and Douglas firs that soar to almost 300 feet. For details on how to find them, you'll have to first find a copy of the *Guide to the Record Trees of British Columbia*, by the late Randy Stoltmann, published by the Western Canada Wilderness Committee (and available at their store in Gastown, see "Secret Environment").

Lighthouse Park, on a gorgeous peninsula with a rocky foreshore (south of Marine Drive in West Vancouver), has some of the largest remaining Douglas firs in the region. And there are more statuesque examples in **Cypress Provincial Park**, above the Upper Levels Highway in West Vancouver, and on **Hollyburn Ridge**, reachable by trail from the Cypress Bowl parking lot.

But if you want to immerse yourself in the ultimate coastal environment, and take in some giant conifers, make your way to North Vancouver's **Capilano River Regional Park**. Drive up Capilano Road, beyond the Capilano Suspension Bridge, and onto Capilano Park Road (it's well posted).

At the end of the road, you'll find the drop-dead gorgeous **Capilano Canyon** — a glacier-carved gorge, filled with dark greenish water that tumbles and eddies through a series of coves, pools, and benignly named "drops." Walk across the wooden suspension bridge and turn right onto a trail that wends a few hundred yards up the hill to a stand of trees with several centuries-old Douglas firs. The largest is said to be eight feet in diameter and more than 200 feet tall. A few yards further and you can see the 295-foot Capilano Dam spillway.

Revel in this mini-exhibit of the coastal rainforest: long-fallen tree trunks or "nurse trees" that support and nurture trees of their own, lovely mosses and lichens covering massive old-growth stumps and rock, and native salal bushes, ferns, and delicate huckleberry (berries in season) — all alongside a vigorous, salmon-spawning river.

SECRET

TROLLEYS AND BUSES

One thing that sets Vancouver apart from most other North American cities is its trolley bus system. Back in the 1950s, as the city began to dismantle its electric streetcar (railway) system, it opted to take advantage of cheap, abundant hydroelectricity, and buy buses that run on overhead wires. Soon, forty-four- and forty-eight-passenger buses built by a Canadian foundry — cream in color and sporting the BC Electric Company "thunderbird logo" — were running along most major thoroughfares.

In the 1980s, when diesel buses where increasingly taking over, BC Transit considered scrapping the trolley fleet. But Vancouverites had become attached to this generally smooth-moving, quiet, and clean form of transportation, and the popular fleet was renewed and expanded. Even at the turn of the twenty-first century, there is talk of ordering more trolley buses — abandonment is no longer an option.

In light of the exorbitant pricetags and endless politics surrounding other transit options, the trolley remains a kind of poor-man's workhorse. It does, though, have disadvantages. For one, it occasionally comes off the rails, and the driver has to get behind the bus and deftly maneuver the trolley poles back onto the overhead wires. And, obviously, it can't go places where there are no wires (new wire-rails were installed out to UBC not long ago).

The second-best transit options are the articulated diesel buses that operate on new rapid-transit B-line routes. While transit engineers are just beginning to make use of all the available rapid-bus technology — bus-stop electronic messaging and traffic-light overrides, for example — the B-lines are hugely popular, largely because they stop only at major intersections and save time. One of the busiest is the #99 Broadway B-line (Commercial Drive to UBC). Another useful B-line, particularly if you're traveling between the airport and downtown Vancouver with limited luggage, is the #98 along Granville Street.

Other good bus routes — for practical and picturesque reasons — are the #22, which loops around east-side Knight Street and west-side Macdonald Street; and the #250 from downtown, via the Lions Gate Bridge, to Dundarave and Horseshoe Bay (the latter is operated by West Vancouver Blue Bus, the Cadillac of BC bus systems).

For more on public transit services, go to www.translink.bc.ca or call 604-953-3333. Detailed timetables of all Lower Mainland bus and SkyTrain routes are available at the Central Branch of the Vancouver Public Library at 350 West Georgia Street.

S E C R E T

24 HOURS
❧

This is not a city known for its late-night life, but it's starting to happen. **The Naam** (see "Secret Vegetarian") is always open. One of the safest (perhaps) and most pleasant places to hang out in the small hours, or anytime, is **Calhoun's Bakery Café** (3035 West Broadway, Kitsilano, 604-737-7062, www.calhouns.bc.ca). This is a large place, successfully decorated on a country log-cabin theme, filled with generous-sized wooden tables at which university students with laptops appear to have settled for good. Good, inexpensive, deli-style food with beer or wine is always available.

If you need a drug store, **Shoppers Drug Mart** and pharmacy (2302 West 4th Avenue, Kitsilano, 604-738-3138; 1125 Davie Street, West End, 604-669-2424; 885 West Broadway, Central Vancouver, 604-708-1135, www.shoppersdrugmart.ca) is always open. On the Internet front, **Star Internet Café** (1690 Robson Street, West End, 604-685-4645) is both a Korean video outlet and a well-equipped English- and Korean-language Internet café. For fitness all-nighters, **Fitness World** (200–1185 Georgia Street, Downtown, 604-662-7774, www.fitnessworld.ca) is open round the clock, Monday through Friday.

SECRET

VEGETARIAN

The Naam (2724 West 4th Avenue, Kitsilano, 604-738-7151, www.thenaam.com) is no secret; indeed, it's Vancouver's oldest and arguably best-loved "natural food" and vegetarian restaurant. It's open around the clock; boasts a delightful patio; and serves wine, beer, and cider, as well as heady desserts such as double-fudge cake and pecan pie. There's also a vast array of soups, melts, Mexican dishes, veggie burgers, and entrées such as fettuccine con aglio e olio. In addition, the Naam serves macrobiotic dishes, and others with no eggs or dairy.

A perennial favorite among vegetarians, and the place for the likes of soy-based mock duck, is the **Buddhist Vegetarian Restaurant** (137 East Pender Street, Chinatown, 604-683-8816).

Another popular spot, a take-out really, is Asia-inspired **Planet Veg** (1941 Cornwall Avenue, Kitsilano, 604-734-1001). This tiny eatery comes up with excellent samosas, burgers, subs, rice-pots, and roti-rolls — the latter served with tamarind chutney.

Sweet Cherubim Natural Foods and Restaurant (1105 Commercial Drive, East Vancouver, 604-253-0969, www.sweetcherubim.com) dishes out inexpensive snacks that run from feta-cheese samosas and wheat-free nachos to hemp-raisin-walnut cookies with organic chai. You get the picture — and the baker's a vegan.

Sejuiced (1958 West 4th Avenue, Kitsilano) is known for its juices and light organic and vegan dishes. And a hip restaurant (in a decidedly downtrodden part of town), with a nice upstairs vibe, is **Radha Yoga & Eatery** (728 Main Street, Downtown Eastside, www.radhavancouver.org). Weekend dining only. A long-timer is small, atmospheric **Annapurna** (1812 West 4th Avenue, Kitsilano, 604-5959, www.annapurnavegetarian.com). It serves Indian vegetarian cuisine, and is licensed.

Quejo's (4129 Main Street, East Vancouver, 604-420-0832, www.quejos.com) specializes in Brazilian-style "cheese-buns," sans wheat and gluten, in "flavors" such as sun-dried tomato, basil, and jalapeño. Little wonder that there's lots of foot traffic here, and that quejos ("kay-hoes") turn up at upscale vegetarian eateries and shops elsewhere, including the wheat- and gluten-free Kitsilano bakery **Panne Rizo** (see "Secret Bakeries").

A vegetarian's destination, **the Foundation** (2301 Main Street, East Vancouver, 604-708-0881) serves great fare (generous portions) at modest prices — with flare. For example, Pesto Imprisoned comprises fresh basil, spinach, peanut pesto and "sheeped" cheeses. It's baked open faced and served with mixed greens. Foundation is licenced.

Budgies Burritos (44 Kingsway, East Vancouver, 604-874-5408) is said to have the best burritos in the city. It also dishes out tacos with tofu-turkey sausage, roasted potatoes, or chipotle tofu at pretty amazing prices.

S E C R E T
VIDEO
❖

Video fans on a budget can do worse than begin their search at the **Vancouver Public Library** (604-331-3603, www.vpl.ca) — primarily the Central Branch (350 West Georgia Street, Downtown) but suburban branches as well. The VPL has a fair video and DVD stock — well, maybe not *Terminator 2* or *The Jane Mansfield Story*, but certainly art-film classics, such as the post-war thriller *The Third Man* (1949, Britain, Orson Welles and Joseph Cotten). And with a library card, acquired with proof of residence, rental costs nothing.

Videomatica remains alternative-film central (1855 West 4th Avenue, Kitsilano, 604-734-0411, www.vidiomatica.bc.ca). The outlet claims to have 20,000 titles (thankfully not all on display). The stock includes a good selection of British TV series and movies. You'll also find US-made black-and-white classics and lesser-known movies from around the world. Helpful employees will direct you to smaller city outlets if you have a particular bent or cultish need they can't address.

There are a number of Chinese and Indian video outlets on the east side — small operations that come and go. On last look, half a dozen outlets on Main and Fraser streets, Kingsway and Victoria Drive are renting and selling Asian — mainly Indian (Bollywood), Cantonese, Mandarin and Filipino — DVDs, videos and CDs.

Eastsiders have a great resource in **Happy Bats Cinema**, a bright space offering 25,000 titles in dvd and Blu-ray. Includes foreign, horror, British, kids, docs, weird cult movies and new releases (2830 Main Street, East Vancouver, 604-877-0666, www.happybatscinema.com).

SECRET
VINTAGE

Vintage is a fancy, abused term used to market old clothing and other collectibles; in reality, we're talking here about a continuum that runs through quality consignment to no-nonsense, ultra-cheap thrift. My goal is to recommend some of the best of a staggering number of outlets, and those with genuinely interesting older clothes.

"Lots of local labels, and plenty of pre-loved and refurbished clothes" is how one patron describes **Mintage**. Both locations (1946 West Fourth Avenue, Kitsilano, 604-646-8243 and 1714 Commercial Drive, East Vancouver, 604-871-0022) are nice spaces, too.

Main Street, between East 17th and 28th avenues — a pleasant stroll — has become Vintage Central, with numerous businesses dealing in vintage, retro, consignment, as well as contemporary clothing and accessories.

A good-looking vintage location is **front and company** (3772 Main Street, East Vancouver, 604-879-8431) — actually an assemblage of storefronts that includes hip collectibles and clothes. It's at Main Street and East 22nd Avenue, among a cluster of clothing shops, a number of them carrying old stuff. On the wild and cluttered site is **Echo** (3288 Main Street, East Vancouver, 604-874-5550); on the other hand, **Lines Clothing** (3793 Main Street, East Vancouver, 604-871-0998) is orderly and shows loads of costume jewelry.

South Granville is a west-side hub, so expect consignment to market mid- to high-end clothing. Reviews are mixed: one of the bigger outlets, **Turnabout** (3109 Granville Street, Central Vancouver, 604-

734-5313; 3112 West Broadway, Kitsilano, 604-731-7762; www.turna-boutclothing.com), carries a lot of stock, well displayed, including major designer labels. The **Blue Unicorn** (3136 Oak Street, Central Vancouver, 604-734-5924), a small store, is all froth and fun — and theatrical: studded black pants for a Mexican night on the town, or a broad-feathered eyepiece for a Venetian carnival.

You'll find an ever-changing cluster of relatively good consignment stores on West 4th Avenue between Collingwood and Alma streets, as well as some on Fourth Avenue in central Kitsilano, and downtown. Check out www.secondhandsavvy.com for the latest locations.

At the decidedly thrifty end of the spectrum there's **Value Village** (1820 East Hastings Street, East Vancouver, 604-254-4282; and 6415 Victoria Drive, South Vancouver, 604-327-4434, www.valuevillage. com). My bohemian cousin has been known to outfit her two young teens there, to great effect. The YWCA runs a great thrift shop in the consignment/vintage heartland (4399 Main Street, East Vancouver, 604-675-9996, www.yweavan.org).

SECRET

VOLLEYBALL
AND ULTY

I've said this before, but I'll reiterate: some Vancouverites think of BC as California North. So it follows that outdoor volleyball is huge. Go to **Kitsilano Beach** on any summer afternoon and you'll see beautifully buffed (and less perfect) bodies reaching for the net (and perhaps wider attention) at a series of courts along the sand.

However, less physically attuned city dwellers — particularly those who live near the city's only really impressive stretches of sandy beach, at Locarno and Spanish Banks — don't like this volleyball incursion one little bit. They've been doggedly fighting to prevent this beach-life phenomenon from moving into their Northwest Marine Drive area — one they feel should remain "family friendly" and au naturel, meaning, in this case, relatively quiet and devoted to nature (as in water and trees).

Less controversially, volleyball is also played on grass. Of course, it also runs indoors year round, mainly at public community centers around the city. You can drop in for a game, attend a course or training clinic, and play in a league.

Vancouver Volleyball (www.vancouvervolleyball. com) covers this territory. Also contact **Volleyball BC** (604-291-2007, www.bcva.ca). And there's a **Vancouver Gay Volleyball Association** with a busy league program (www.vgva.com).

Volleyball is also center court at the web site of the city-based sport and social club dubbed **Urban Rec** (www.urbanrec.ca, 604-879-9800). But the club also offers hockey, kayaking, Ultimate, and the more challenging sport of socializing.

Ultimate — sometimes referred to as "Ulty" — is popular. This practice of flinging a plastic disc — and ideally leaping and catching it — is accompanied by the deeply held philosophy that the world would be a better place if people were less hung up on regulations and hyper-competition. Ultimate goals and technical infractions are generally sorted out among the players; self-policing and honest reporting is germane to the sport. At the conclusion of the game, players usually come out with a goofy song or bit of doggerel. (They must be exhausted; this is phenomenal exercise on various fronts.) Leagues, including coed ones, run year round. For everything you need to know, visit www.vul.bc.ca.

SECRET

WALKS WITH CLAPHAM

No books have turned conventional wisdom on walking in and around this city on its head like those written by retired mathematician Charles Clapham.

A former city councilor and veteran urban walker called Clapham's second book, *Walk the Burrard Loop*, "the most subversive book I've read about the Vancouver region in years.

"Though the most commonly used words in the book are 'left' and 'right,'" wrote Gordon Price, "it demolishes the boundaries of parochialism regardless of political stripe. After close reading, you will never see the region the same [way] again."

This and other books, *Walk Horseshoe Bay to the USA* and *Walk the Fraser: Vancouver to Mission*, are collectively published as *Great Walks of Vancouver: The Lower Mainland at Your Feet* (Granville Island Publishing; available at most Vancouver bookstores).

What Clapham had done is devise entirely new walking routes — really a series of daily walks that, if completed, make for a memorable collective experience and show off the region at its natural best.

Importantly, *Great Walks* shows how you can walk in one direction and return by public transit — an almost subversive suggestion, as Price notes, in this auto-dependent culture. Further, every walk is described in copious detail — with a map, distances (down to a fraction of a kilometer), and the projected time it will take. Bits of history, ecology, politics, and whatever help you understand and enjoy the landscape.

Walk Horseshoe Bay to the USA follows the West Vancouver shoreline, around the Point Grey peninsula to South Vancouver, and on to Richmond, Tsawwassen, Boundary Bay, and White Rock. *Walk the Burrard Loop* begins downtown, then follows North Vancouver's waterworn landscapes of Mosquito and Lynn creeks to Burnaby Mountain, the Coquitlam and Pitt rivers, and back to Burnaby Lake Park and Vancouver's Renfrew Ravine. Walks average eight or nine miles.

Price, who walked the Burrard Loop, added: "Vancouver...is a profoundly rural city, though you'd never know it from the front seat of an SUV. Clapham reveals how you can better experience the farthest parts of this region more conveniently if you don't use a car."

Clapham's newest book is *Walk Squamish to Whistler* — six "relatively easy" one-day hikes through the valley system that includes the spectacular Cheakamus River, canyon and falls (Walk #3), but also (on other walks) Brackendale and the eagle run, lovely little Lucille Lake for warm-water swimming, the old Pemberton Trail to the Callaghan River suspension bridge and the Valley Trail through Alpha Lake Park. This booklet is available at the Squamish Adventure Centre, off the Sea-to-Sky Highway, and other outlets. For more info and trail updates, www.greatwalksofvancouver.com.

S E C R E T

WEDDINGS

There are those among us who hanker to witness a wedding party all done up in rented tuxes and six-of-a-kind dresses, a resplendent bride in innocent white, etc., etc. You know who you are. One place to find them is **Queen Elizabeth Park** (off Cambie Street and West 33rd Avenue, Central Vancouver) on any pleasant Saturday afternoon between May and October.

If it's blazingly sunny, prepare for a crush. You're likely to see a wedding party in particularly fancy attire; affairs dripping with jewels and other expressions of wealth; and humdrum family collectives, all confusion, trailing grandparents and chaotic children. The professional photographers will be plotting their time and space in one of the park's two lovely steep-walled former rock quarries, filled with grass, gardens, and romantic draws such as a small footbridge. So great is the demand for prime picture-taking locations that you may have the pleasure of witnessing a nasty dispute simmering — just below the surface, of course. If you'd like to join the fray, you can buy handmade wedding gowns on themes running from medieval to Victorian at **Venus & Mars Universal Clothing** (315 Cambie Street, Downtown, 604-687-1908, www.venusandmars.biz). Owner Sanné Lambert has been making these "ethereal robes of velvet, embossed, Gothic styles" for more than a decade. While she sells for grads and formals, weddings are her big market.

Still in this category, **The House Gallery Boutique** (2865 West 4th Avenue, Kitsilano, 604-732-8647, www.velvetandlace.com) sells gorgeous vintage and ready-to-wear, and makes Tudor and Victorian apparel to order.

SECRET

WILDLIFE
❧

There's no other place in the world, I'm certain, where you can witness wild grizzly bears hibernating their way through winter in a den designed to replicate the dry log they might otherwise chose as their seasonal nest — and just a dozen feet away from busy ski trails.

At the **Grouse Mountain Refuge for Endangered Wildlife** (North Vancouver, 604-984-0661, www.grousemountain.com), you can see four fast-growing orphaned bears via hidden infrared camera (now a lumbering 600 to 900 pounds each). In winter, they're snoozing and consuming their excess fat. When the bears emerge in spring, you can watch them playing in the snow, eating berries, and generally messing about their forest retreat. Bears will be bears.

Run by wildlife veterinarian Ken Macquisten, the refuge was established after two cubs, Coola and Grinder, were found abandoned and starving in the wilderness of coastal and southeast BC respectively. They're now fully grown. Coola is easy-going and introverted. He loves water, and can be found for the most of the summer up to his neck in the pond. Grinder is outgoing and high-spirited, and prefers to scrutinize the visitors. Together they spend up to four months hibernating in a rustic retreat. In spring they step back into their large wilderness habit, one with little human intervention. A goal of the program is to find ways to return orphaned grizzlies into the wild.

Grouse Mountain also lets fly highly skilled birds of prey — falcons, eagles, and hawks — in free-flight demonstrations daily from June to September. It recently added a juvenile Spotted Owl, as part of a program to breed and rebuilt the endangered specie.

SECRET

WROUGHT IRON
❧

For wrought-iron enthusiasts among us, must-sees are the galleries (as in "covered passageways") at the center of the **Burrard Street Bridge**. This is arguably the finest of the city's several dozen bridges — after the Lions Gate, of course. Walk the bridge on a sunny day, and the black-metal curlicues and arrows will cast elegant shadows on the ochre-colored tower of this Art Deco structure, opened in 1932. The bridge connects the downtown peninsula with Kitsilano to the south, and provides unsurpassable views of Burrard Inlet, Howe Sound, and the coastal mountains. While you're on it, look upward for the prow-posted busts of George Vancouver, who sailed into Burrard Inlet on June 12, 1792, and fellow captain Harry Burrard, with whom Vancouver messed about the West Indies in 1785.

SECRET

X-FILES
❧

Gotta admit to bypassing *x-Files*, but there are millions out there who remember the 1993–2001 television series with David Duchovny and Gillian Anderson as one of the finest film odysseys ever made. Of 201 episodes, 117 were shot in Vancouver.

Vancouver Sun television critic Alex Strachan says that a key to the success of the series involving the paranormal, and a factor in its

demise after it finally relocated to Los Angeles, was the Vancouver setting: "The mist, the rain, the soft, pale light and cold, damp air that created its own eerie special effect of people being able to see their breath as they spoke..."

Years after its cancellation, *X-Files* continues to run worldwide; Strachan hints at cult status. Boyd McConnell's **Pendrell Estates** (1419 Pendrell Street, West End, 604-609-2770, www.vancouvermovietours.com), the pretty brick complex where Anderson (aka Special Agent Dana Scully) holed up in the series, continues to attract attention. "People love Hollywood," reminds McConnell, whose apartment building has since been the subject of features for 60 Hollywood productions. And movie-makers and tourists continue to book into the none-too-cheap apartment-hotel; McDonnell knows the scene. Not only does he provide tours of his own set, he shows people to this and other movie locations around the city.

However, if you'd rather suss out *X-Files* locations on your own, here's some of the others: Fox Mulder (Duchovny) lived in a stalwart brick building called The Wellington (1630 York Avenue, Kitsilano) and Mulder's father lived at 6476 Blenheim Street on the Westside. The uninspiring BC Hydro building (333 Dunsmuir Street, Downtown) served as the lobby for the FBI, as did the home of our two major daily newspapers, Granville Square (200 Granville Street, Downtown).

The Robson Square Conference Centre, a partly underground complex now used as a satellite campus by UBC, functioned as NASA mission control. The Plaza of Nations, at 770 Pacific Boulevard, somehow passed muster as Miami International Airport (minus the runways). Poor old 1190 Homer Street was assigned to play the Texas Book Depository, and Pacific Central Station (1150 Station Street, Central Vancouver) played the role of Bronx Station, New York.

SECRET

YOGA

Yoga is huge—indeed, it's been said that you can't amble through Kitsilano without pumping into a yoga mat. Kits-based **Semperviva** (www.semperviva.com) has four studios, including a light-flooded space on Granville Island, overlooking False Creek. It offers Ashtanga, Hatha, Kundalini, Power, Prenatal and Yin yoga at four locations. The **Bikram Yoga College of India** has several studios (including 2681 West Broadway, Kitsilano, 604-742-3830, www.bikramyoga.com). And most city-run community centers (www.vancouver.ca/parks) offer yoga, as does the downtown YWCA (535 Hornby Street, Downtown, 604-895-5777, www.ywcahealthandfitness.com).

SECRET FUTURE

No tour guide can be definitively comprehensive, especially when the aim is to uncover those hidden places that have previously escaped notice. Undoubtedly, some worthwhile attractions have remained hidden even from our best efforts to ferret them out.

In the interest of our own self-improvement, we ask readers to let us know of the places they've unearthed that they believe warrant inclusion in future editions of *Secret Vancouver*. If we use your suggestion, we'll send you a free copy on publication. Please contact us at the following address:

Secret Vancouver
c/o ECW PRESS

2120 Queen Street East, Suite 200
Toronto, Ontario, Canada M4E 1E2

Or e-mail us at: info@ecwpress.com

PHOTO SITES

FRONT COVER: Inukshuk and English Bay
BACK COVER: UBC Museum of Anthropology

SUBJECT INDEX

Fashion/Clothing/Accessories

Festivals

History/Heritage/Time

Markets and Malls

Music

Nightlife/Scene

Snacks/Light Meals

LOCATION INDEX

Gastown

Granville Island 124–26

ALPHABETICAL INDEX